SEA LIFE
of the Pacific Northwest

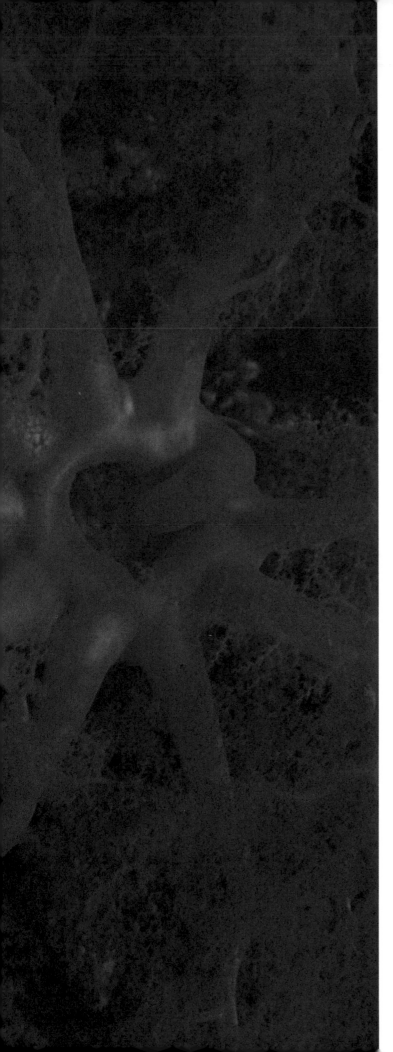

SEA LIFE
of the Pacific Northwest

Stefani Hewlett
Assistant to Curator, Vancouver Public Aquarium

K. Gilbey Hewlett
Curator, Vancouver Public Aquarium

Illustrations by
Greg Davies

With the support of the Vancouver Public Aquarium
Murray A. Newman
Director

McGraw-Hill Ryerson Limited
*Toronto Montreal New York London Sydney Auckland
Johannesburg Düsseldorf Mexico Panama São Paulo
Singapore Kuala Lumpur New Delhi*

For Brooke

All photographs not credited to particular photographers are from
the collections of Stefani Hewlett, K. Gilbey Hewlett and the
Vancouver Public Aquarium.
ISBN 0-07-082336-7
1 2 3 4 5 6 7 8 9 0 BP 5 4 3 2 1 0 9 8 7 6

Printed and bound in Canada

Contents

Preface

Life is everywhere — in the soil, in the skies, on the land and in the sea. Never before has this awareness affected so many, and never before has there been the knowledge that much of this life can be or has been lost. Living things of all kinds are taken less for granted today than yesterday. People want to know.

Through our experience working with the public at the Vancouver Public Aquarium, camping, talking with boaters, divers, fishermen and families out enjoying the beach at low tide, we became aware of the tremendous interest and desire of the lay person to know about what they were seeing and the problems they encountered in trying to find information. So often we were asked, "Where can I get a good book on ——?"

Many excellent publications are available on various aspects of marine life of the Pacific Northwest. However, too many of these take for granted a good grounding in biology and are therefore difficult for the lay person to use easily, being technical in nature and aimed at communicating important information to other students of biology.

There was a need for a book on the marine life of the area which would guide the reader to identify what was seen and provide some insight into the natural history of the organism. How big does it grow? What does it eat? Why does it live here? How does it reproduce? Which are its enemies? Can it be eaten? Does it bite?

The present book attempts to fill this need and stimulate questions in the mind of the observer. A representation of commonly encountered marine forms from sea plants to whales is included, with the exception of sea birds which are well documented in other books.

This book does not pretend to be a definitive work on the marine organisms of the area; it does attempt to be accurate and readable for the audience it was written for — the fisherman, the boater, the camper, the beach walker, the diver, anyone who has seen the teeming life of a Pacific tide pool, and marvelled at it.

ACKNOWLEDGMENTS

The preparation of this work has been a great adventure for us both. Most rewarding has been the interest, generosity and support of so many colleagues and friends. To these and to our family we wish to extend thanks and gratitude that words alone cannot express.

To Dr. Murray A. Newman, Director par excellence of the Vancouver Public Aquarium, we are grateful for reading the manuscript; without his support the opportunity for writing this book would not have come about.

To Dr. Pierre Dow, not only for his photographs and long hours in the darkroom and in the field on our behalf, but for his enthusiasm and good-humored criticism we extend special thanks. To Ron Long of Simon Fraser University for his photographs and his care and skill in processing so many pictures, and to all the individuals who so generously allowed us to use their photographs: Jim Willoughby and John Quail of Willoughby's Divers' Den; John Ketcheson of the Nanaimo Biological Station; Finn Larsen, John Ford and John Allen of the Vancouver Public Aquarium; Don Kramer of the Fisheries Research Board, Vancouver; Dr. Peter Fankboner of Simon Fraser University; Charles Farwell of the Scripps Aquarium-Museum; Ray Bauer of the Scripps Institute of Oceanography; Graham Ellis of the Arctic Biological station; Martin Roberts, Hans Meyer, Jeff Stewart, and Tony Pletcher.

A very special thanks to Duane and Martha Goertson for notes and special collection. Without the help of Mike Gray and the Goertsons many interesting animals would not have been illustrated. For algae identification we are indebted to Dr. Ron Foreman and Thomas Mumford, Jr., of the University of British Columbia, and for shells, Dr. Watson Mac-Crostie of the Centennial Museum, Vancouver.

To Marilyn Dow for typing and proofreading, to Barbara Dow, not only for packing equipment and cameras under the most adverse conditions, but for maintaining a cheerful disposition more precious than rubies, we extend our thanks.

No small feat has been the hours of typing necessary to prepare the manuscript for publication. We appreciate enormously the time devoted and the great patience of Janet McCloy who faced reams of illegible copy with quiet resignation; and Lynne Allies we thank for her typing, proofreading and genuine interest in the project and what it is trying to do. We thank Pat Graffin who typed the final manuscript, and without whose special talent for finding a spelling error faster than a speeding bullet much would have been lost.

A great debt is owed to Greg Davies for his exquisite illustrations and spirit of cooperation; to Dr. Dean Fisher of the University of British Columbia for his reading and supportive comments on the Marine Mammal section; and to Dr. Bill Austin for giving us the benefit of his tremendous knowledge and his time in reading and commenting on the Invertebrate section. Dr. Austin's taped remarks were not only constructive and informative but highly entertaining.

In closing, we must thank our son Brooke, whose joy in discovery at the seashore has been a constant inspiration.

STEFANI I. HEWLETT
K. GILBEY HEWLETT

Introduction

THE WATER PLANET

Ours is a water planet and as such is perhaps unique in the solar system. Except in the polar regions, the Earth's average surface temperature falls within the exceedingly narrow range between 0° and 100° C. (32° – 212° F.) where water remains liquid. At lower temperatures, water becomes solid ice, at higher ones, a gas.

Over 70 percent of the earth's surface is covered in water, over 330 million cubic miles. If all the earth's irregularities were smoothed out, both above and below the water, there would be no land at all — the ocean would cover the entire globe to a depth of 3,660 meters (12,000 feet). Land's tallest peak, Mount Everest, 8,253.5 meters (29,028 feet.) could be sunk without a trace in the ocean's greatest abyss, the 10,863-meter (35,630-foot)-deep Marianas Trench in the Western Pacific.

It is no wonder, then, that the gravitational pull of the sun and moon will have an observable effect on such an enormous mass of liquid. The phenomenon is known to us all as the twice daily rise and fall of the tides. As the moon swings around the earth every twenty-four hours, a bulge of water appears on the side of the earth facing the moon and at the same time an equal bulge forms on the opposite side. The sun, because it is so very far away, has about one-half the pulling effect of the moon. However, it is still able to reinforce, or offset, the moon's pull according to its relative position. For example, when the sun and moon are in line — as in the full moon — they act together producing unusually high and low tides, known as "spring" tides. During the summer in the Pacific Northwest these occur during the day, whereas during December extreme tides occur at night. When the moon, sun and earth are at right angles to each other, as in the moon's first and third quarters, the pull of the sun and moon cancel each other producing tides of low amplitude known as "neap" tides.

Tides are also influenced by the shape of the ocean basins and the enclosed land masses. Islands occurring near the center of their tidal basins, like the Island of Tahiti, have little tidal action (30.5 centimeters [1 foot]), whereas tides near the rim of a tidal basin have greater tidal differences, as in the Pacific Northwest where the greatest tidal difference averages 4.6 meters (15 feet).

The sea is not, as it was once thought to be, one great teeming breadbasket of fish. The vast majority of marine organisms are tied to the shore, continental shelf regions and the surface of the sea. Once past the continental shelf, the sea bottom falls away rapidly to the deep abyss and darkness. In the relative shallows and at the surface, the density and total volume of living organisms is greatest because the food for all marine animals is ultimately derived from marine plants. As most plants can thrive only where there is adequate light for photosynthesis, the deeper the water the less sunlight penetrates, fewer plants grow and, therefore, the less there is to eat for herbivorous animals and the animals that, in turn, feed on them.

Marine animals are generally described as *plankton, nekton* and *benthos*. The first named comprises all those small drifting organisms, both plant and animal, which have only feeble powers of locomotion and are carried helplessly at the mercy of currents and tides. Nekton refers to strong-swimming animals such as squid, fishes and whales, whose movements are powerful enough to make them independent of water movements to a considerable degree. Benthos embraces all those bottom-living organisms, such as clams, starfish and sponges, which crawl over the substrate, burrow into it, are sedentary in habitat, or remain fixed to one spot.

THE REGION OF THE PACIFIC NORTHWEST

It does not take much to realize that many fish and invertebrates found in the Pacific Northwest will be different from those in the tropics or in polar seas, or even from those of the Japanese coast though the latitude is about the same.

A primary factor in the distributional differences of flora (plant) and fauna (animal) is temperature. There exists an extraordinary uniformity of temperature, 14-15° C (55-59° F), from northern Baja California, to Alaska — in other words, the Pacific Northwest coastal region. This is the result of currents; the West Wind Drift, moving in the Pacific Ocean from west to east. On reaching the west coast of North America, the current splits to the north and south. Upwelling cold water mixes with the coastal currents off California and results in water temperatures uniform enough to enable many species of plants and animals to live throughout the length of the cool-temperate Pacific Northwest region.

Along the coast of British Columbia and Washington there also exists a mixing of northern and southern populations which find the northern limits of their range in this area, and northern Alaskan species which find the southern limits of their range here too.

Distribution is not limited by temperature alone, but is affected by water quality (the degree of salinity and oxygen content); by physical barriers in the form of underwater valleys and mountains; by predators and by competitors, to name just a few.

Even within an area of uniform water quality and temperature, there will be a distribution of plants and animals according to habitat. Hardy species such as rockweed or shore crabs, able to withstand the rigors of exposure during low tide, are found in the "intertidal" region. Some species, such as the moon snail, thrive in sandy areas, whereas the majority of marine organisms are adapted to a rocky habitat that provides a solid place of attachment or offers protection behind and under rocks. Exposure and wave shock must also be taken into account. Animals, such as the surf anemone, are adapted to withstand the full force of unbridled waves, whereas some delicate hy-droids would be crushed and torn by only one great wave.

Plants and animals live where they do because they are adapted to a particular environment: the water quality; the availability of food; the opportunity to reproduce successfully; and the relationship they have with other plants and animals sharing the environment.

No plant or animal can exist as a thing unto itself; all are interrelated and therefore interdependent. If an environment remains stable the organisms within it coexist in a balanced state. When the environment is changed through natural events or conditions, such as volcanic eruptions, altered currents, etc., or through man-made changes such as sewage disposal, breakwaters, and so on, the balance is upset and the plants and animals must readjust their life styles — some go, some stay, according to each species' capacity to adapt. For example, off the coast of California, sewage entering the sea provided nutrients for increased algae growth, which set the scene for a sea urchin population explosion. More food for the urchins meant more urchins survived. Soon an army of urchins marched on the great brown kelp beds, chewing away the kelp where it was attached to the sea bottom. As the large seaweeds became detached they floated away, taking with them the sheltered habitat of many juvenile sports fish species. Later came fishermen and there were few fish to catch because man's own wastes had destroyed the fish nurseries.

The reader should bear in mind, however, that living things are always changing. The factors which provided for the evolution and demise of the giant 91.4-meter (100-foot) shark and the dinosaur still exist. Just as many of the earth's living organisms were different two million years ago, so they will likely be as different again two million years hence.

Enjoy, enjoy, and take care at the beach, on the boat, in the water. Consider yourself a guest of the marine life of the Pacific Northwest. Be patient, turn

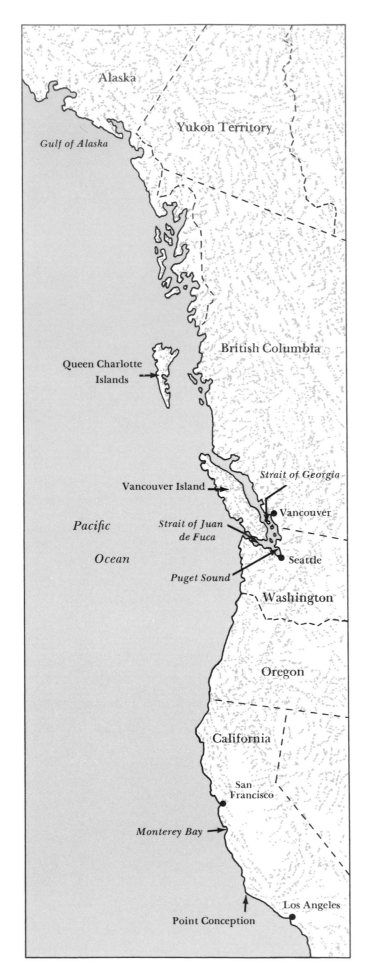

over rocks, sit quietly by a tide pool and observe through your own shadow the community below busy with the business of survival.

Please remember that carelessness or thoughtlessness may mean needless death. If a rock is lifted or turned, replace it the way it was found, otherwise some small creature may fry or freeze in a few short minutes. Fill back clam holes, never disturb eggs of any kind. By all means enjoy the sea's bounty, but take only what can be eaten. Abide by size and catch limits set down by fish and wildlife agencies; they have been invoked for your own future enjoyment, to ensure an abundance of animals for everyone.

If you are not a diver, visit your local aquarium and see, in dryness and comfort, another dimension of marine fauna.

SCIENTIFIC AND COMMON NAMES

For many laymen and even many students of biology, the whole business of naming creatures is a colossal headache. There is no problem, really, in naming a particular plant or animal by any name which one feels is appropriate. There is no law to say that a dandelion cannot be called a whisker ball or anything else. Anyone is able to exercise individual creativity and inspiration in naming plants and animals, just as we do in naming our children or cats, dogs and canaries. However, do not expect to be able to communicate with others regarding the organism so named. From family to family, community to community, country to country, the common or vernacular names applied to living organisms change.

Many years ago, starting with the Swedish biologist Linnaeus, scientists began a standardized system of naming all living organisms, both plant and animal. In most cases two Latinized names are given. The first refers to genus (a taxonomic group) and the second to species. For example, *Felis domesticus* is a domestic cat. *Felis concolor* is the cougar, and *Felis nigripes* is the African black-footed cat. *Felis* indicates the close

relationship of the three cats; *domesticus, concolor* and *nigripes* distinguishes each species as being separate and unique.

Scientific names are used to avoid confusion, as happens with widely used common names. For example, many North American species were given their common names by European pioneers settling in the New World. When a fish looking and behaving much like the Atlantic salmon was seen on the Pacific coast, it was named "salmon" and is still known by that name today. However, the two fish are not the same. The former is *Salmo salar* and the latter are really five different species of the genus *Oncorhynchus*.

The establishment of scientific names is subject to stringent rules and comes under the authority of an international congress, as opposed to even widely accepted common names which are changeable and changed for all manner of reasons. A case in point is the longjaw rockfish (*Sebastes alutus*). A number of years ago, a commercial fishery was formed to market the species as frozen fishsticks. Sold under the name Longjaw Rockfish, sales were poor. Marketing analysts established that poor sales were not due to appearance or palatability, so they advised that the fish be renamed Pacific Ocean Perch. Now, Pacific Ocean Perch (*Sebastes alutus*), alias longjaw rockfish, sells well, averaging 15,000 metric tons, or tonnes (33 million pounds) per year — which only goes to prove that while a rose smells as sweet by any other name, the consumer likes some names more than others.

Bull kelp (Nereocystis leutkeana). The complete plant, including stipe and blades, may grow to 30 m (100 ft.). The bulb contains enough carbon monoxide to kill a chicken in one minute. It serves as a float to keep the large blades near the water's surface and obtain good access to sunlight.

Seaweeds

Algae and sea grasses

The toothpaste used to brush your teeth this morning, the last dish of ice cream you ate, and even the mayonnaise in your lunch sandwich more than likely contained some by-product of marine algae. More commonly known as seaweeds, the marine algae are pillars of the marine community. Their commercial uses are important but their biological function is essential, directly or indirectly, to all life in the sea and to land animals as well. Algae are found in all oceans of the world, ranging from the minute floating plants (*phytoplankton*) to giant kelps — an incredible diversity in size, shape and habitat.

PHYTOPLANKTON

Some concept of the nature and function of the microscopic algae is essential for an understanding of the marine community. These tiny plants, along with tiny animals, including larval or egg forms of many species such as starfish, clams, anemones, et cetera, collectively are known as plankton (from the Greek *planktos*, "drifting"). Plankton refers to all free-floating and suspended organisms that drift passively in the water. A huge portion of this plankton is plant material and is called *phytoplankton*. These phytoplankters are so small, dozens would cover the head of a pin. It has been estimated that 4,000 tons of microscopic vegetable matter per square mile is produced annually in the English Channel.

Because phytoplankters are plants, they are able (with the aid of a green pigment called chlorophyll, and sunlight) to convert nutrients dissolved in the sea into organic matter. This is known as *photosynthesis*. As the energy derived from sunlight is essential to this process, the phytoplankton must live within the top layers of ocean water where sufficient sunlight can penetrate.

Photosynthesis in all plants creates oxygen. Phytoplankton growing in huge ocean meadows is producing oxygen, releasing it to the air, constantly renewing the oxygen supply being used by other organisms including man. If the oceans were to become polluted to the point where the phytoplankton was destroyed, in no way could land-dwelling plants produce enough oxygen through their photosynthesis to sustain life.

All animals eat either plants or other animals which have, in turn, eaten plants. In the sea a salmon will perhaps eat a herring, but what does the herring eat? The herring eats the *zooplankton* (the animal organisms of plankton), in the form of tiny shrimps and larvae. In turn, the zooplankton eats the phytoplankton and the phytoplankton produces its own food. This is a very simple example of a "food chain." In any food chain, plants form the foundation.

The phytoplankton, besides being producers of food, are essential recyclers of matter. Animal and vegetable wastes are broken down in the sea by bacteria, creating a kind of fertilizer. Upwelling currents and turbulence bring these nutrients to the waters' surface where they can be utilized by the microscopic plants and, so again, become part of the food chain and what is called natural balance. This process of bacteria breaking down waste products and neutralizing their toxic, or poisonous, effects is utilized in home aquaria where a sub-sand or "biological" filter is used.

The phenomenon known as *red tide* occurs when conditions enable particular species of phytoplankton (*Gonyaulax catanella* on the Pacific coast) to reproduce and become so dense as to discolor the water with red, brown or yellow stain. Concentrations can reach from five hundred thousand to two million per gallon. This generally occurs in areas of upwelling (bottom water moving to the surface), where vast amounts of nutrients are being brought to the ocean's surface, and where sufficiently high surface temperatures occur. This creates a temporary imbalance, the zooplankton being unable to graze the phytoplankton at the rate it is being produced. Animals, such as oysters and clams, which feed by filtering phytoplankton and other small organisms from the water, tend to concentrate in their bodies the toxin produced by the phytoplankton.

Sargassum weed (Sargassum muticum) occurs in the lower intertidal and upper subtidal from British Columbia to Oregon. The long — to 2 m (6.5 ft.) — and profusely branched plants provide shelter for many juvenile fish. This species was introduced from Japan.

Rockweed (Fucus sp.) is a very common seaweed of the middle and lower intertidal zone. When sexually mature, the tips of the plant become swollen. Rockweed grows to 50 cm (20 in.) and is lime or yellowish-green in color.

Pierre Dow

When a human being eats these oysters or clams, the cumulative effect of the toxin affects the central nervous system, resulting in great pain and discomfort.

A red tide is more likely to occur during the summer months and is a temporary phenomenon. As the phytoplankton bloom and multiply they soon use up the nutrients specific to their needs and the balance drops back to normal.

ALGAE

Algae are the plants of the sea, but they differ vastly from land plants, which reproduce from seed. Land plants have established systems which are much more involved than those of algae. They have roots to absorb water and minerals from the soil, stems which conduct these supplies, and leaves which manufacture food (by photosynthesis, from chlorophyll, sunlight and the minerals) to support the entire plant. Algae, on the other hand, have no such sophisticated system.

Photosynthesis, in the algae, takes place over the entire surface of the plant. Their "holdfast," which can be rootlike in appearance, acts simply as an anchor. Their "stipe" is often stemlike in appearance, but performs no transport function, and their "laminae," or blades, which may look like leaves, are not dependent on these other parts for food supply because the entire organism is in intimate and uniform contact with its environment, the sea. (In some of the large kelps there may be some transport from photosynthetic to nonphotosynthetic areas of the plant.)

J. Willoughby

Many algae, in fact, bear no resemblance at all to our usual concept of plants. Some look like spongy, bulbous masses or encrusting growths on rocks. Others are masses of fine threads, drifting freely with the waves.

Many algae are cosmopolitan in their distribution, while others are specific to generalized climatic zones (Arctic, Temperate, Subtropical and Tropical) and particular conditions within those zones. Vertical distribution is dependent on tide, depth, competition and sunlight. In the Pacific Northwest, the turbidity of the water and angle of the sun's rays do not allow sufficient light penetration much beyond 30 meters (100 feet) for algae growth. Further south in the tropics, with more direct sun and reduced turbidity,

there is an abundance of algae at four times this depth.

Algae differ markedly in their ability to withstand the effects of exposure: drying, freezing and temperature change. Those with the greatest tolerance are found in the "intertidal" zone. This is the shore area regularly covered with sea water and left exposed as the tide swells and recedes. Some, such as the stubby 20-millimeter (¾-inch) -high *Prasiola*, are so hardy as to exist above the high tide mark in the splash zone. Some species live in the "subtidal" zone and are always covered with water.

Yet, even in the subtidal zone, attached algae will be found close to shore. As the land falls away, the ocean floor becomes increasingly deeper and therefore darker, unsuitable for the manufacture of food by

15

Sea lettuce (Ulva lactuca) is a common species of the upper intertidal zone. It ranges from Chile to the Bering Sea.

Sea sac (Halosaccion glandiforme) is common and abundant at the mid-tide level. Each individual hollow sac is filled with water and may grow from 10 to 25 cm (4 to 10 in.) in height. Color may vary from yellow-brown, olive to reddish-purple.

Pierre Dow

photosynthesis. The horizontal distribution of algae is dependent upon salinity, degree of exposure, and nature of the substrate. Shore areas near fresh-water outfalls from rivers such as the Fraser River in southern British Columbia are relatively impoverished in terms of marine vegetation. This is due to increased turbidity and reduced salinity (the amount of salts in solution), the result of fresh-water dilution. Exposure is important. It takes a very sturdy seaweed, like the large kelps, to withstand the crashing surf of open coasts. Seaweeds of the open coast are generally firm, with strong holdfasts and thick stipes; yet elastic enough to give with the unharnessed seas. Less hardy species favor protected inshore areas like the rocky shores north of Nanaimo, on the east side of Vancouver Island. Here, protection, plus high salinity, creates an ideal environment for luxuriant forests of algae.

Even more critical is the quality of the substrate or bottom. Sand and loose pebbles offer no security for attachment or anchorage, while large or firm rocks are ideal. It should be mentioned that many species are epiphytic; that is, they attach themselves to other attached algae, though they are not parasitic. This makes identification much more challenging.

Algae are grouped into divisions on the basis of color: green (*Chlorophyceae*), brown (*Phaeophyceae*), red (*Rhodophyceae*), and blue-green (*Myxophytacea*). The green pigment, chlorophyll, is present in all algae but masked by other pigments in all but the greens. Green algae more commonly occur in fresh water and in damp soil. They are far less prevalent in the sea. Commonly seen is the beautiful emerald green sea lettuce (*Ulva lactuca*) which looks very much like its name. Brown algae are the most strictly marine of all seaweeds, with only three small fresh-water forms. Characteristic of exposed shores, brown algae dominate the vegetation of coastal waters in volume, numbers and size, though not in number of species. Most obvious and well-known of these are the kelps like bull or ribbon kelp (*Nereocystis*). In Europe the term

Sea palm (Postelsia palmaeformis) *is a species of upper tidal, exposed coasts and heavy surf. It grows to 60 cm (24 in.) in height. Stripe and holdfast are perennial, whereas blades are renewed each year.*

Giant kelp (Macrocystis intergrifolia) *has individual fronds along its stipe, each supported by its own small float. The plant may grow to 30 m (100 ft.) in length and is perennial, living from four to seven years. As the species occurs in areas of high salinity close to the open sea, yet not directly exposed to heavy surf, beds of giant kelp are an important habitat for many species of young fishes. This species is harvested commercially for algal derivatives.*

"kelp" is applied to the burnt ash of seaweeds, while in North America kelp refers to the large laminar algae such as bull kelp and giant kelp (*Macrocystis*).

The great kelp beds provide a vital service to the marine community, hosting dozens of "roomers" along their blades and stipes. The 30-meter (100-foot) -long *Macrocystis* is the highrise of downtown marine land, offering an offshore home, in well-aerated water, away from overcrowding on the beach. For boaters, the kelp beds mark dangerous underwater shoals and indicate the direction and speed of currents.

The large bulb of bull or ribbon kelp and bulblike structures on other kelps and seaweeds act as flotation devices, ensuring that the plant will lie near the water's surface and obtain sufficient sunlight. One such algae has been called the oyster thief (*Colpomeniasi nuosa*). This balloon-like plant attaches its holdfast to the shells of oysters, inflates its bulb with gases during low tide and carries the oyster with it as it floats away at high tide.

Another very common brown seaweed is rockweed (*Fucus*), also known as popping wrack, a much branched, flattened seaweed. When the plant is reproducing its tips become swollen. This species grows to 30 centimeters (12 inches) in length. Free-floating or attached sargassum or Japanese weed (*Sargassum muticum*) is infamous among anglers but serves as valuable nursery space for many young fishes. This brown algae is an introduced species, having flourished on the west coast after introduction with the Japanese oyster. Sargassum weed is remarkably similar to an indigenous seaweed, the woody chain bladder (*Cystoseira germinata*), which can be distinguished

*Eelgrass (*Zostera* marina) is characteristic of quiet waters in protected bays. Eelgrass beds are important spawning and nursery areas for many species of fish and invertebrates. When in flower, both male and female blooms occur in the same cluster.*

from the introduced plant by its pointed bladders or air sacs. Those of sargassum are always rounded.

Red algae are abundant in terms of species, though not as obvious in numbers. Of the multitude of red species, fewer are found in the cool, temperate and subarctic regions of the Pacific Northwest, yet these tend to be proportionately larger in size than their southern cousins. An easily recognized red alga, is the red rock crust (*Lithothamnium*). Looking much like a splotch of red paint, 2.5 to 10 centimeters (1 to 4 inches) in diameter, it is a stony encrustation, and can vary considerably in color from whitish-pink to deep purple. Another, dulse, or red kale (*Rhodymenia palmata*), is a dull red, irregularly divided, broad blade plant, having a texture like thin rubber. This seaweed is widely used as food or medicine. Dulse is said to make a tasty relish and can be eaten raw, chewed like gum.

Blue-green algae are rather inconspicuous in the marine environment as they are largely microscopic and seen generally as dark, slimy masses.

When looking for algae, then, one should venture out at or just before low tide, to rocky areas away from fresh-water outflows. Surge channels between rocks are very often ideal and will reward the seeker with an Ali Baba's cave of seaweeds and intertidal creatures. As many algae are annuals, in that the blades and stipes grow anew in the spring, while the holdfast is perennial, a fresher, less wave-worn specimen will be found in early summer than in late fall.

The seaweeds provide an excellent subject for collection, preservation and study as they neither bite nor flee from the collector. Algae specimens may be preserved in three to four percent commercial formalin (neutralized with borax) in sea water and kept in a darkened area to preserve color. Some of the very delicate varieties lend themselves well to drying and pressing. Partial drying in the sun, to the consistency of leather, then further slow drying between paper, will usually yield a most attractive design. Special herbarium papers and blotters are available for those wishing to take the extra effort for a more professional mount.

If collecting is not your interest, you may perhaps wish to experiment with a variety of food dishes using seaweed. The Japanese use over twenty varieties in their culinary art. While not all local species may be palatable, none are known to be poisonous. It remains a matter of taste. The nutritional value of seaweeds lies in their mineral and vitamin content. Their Vitamin B (thiamin) content compares favorably with that of many fruits and vegetables. However, since most of the algae's complex carbohydrates (17 to 60 percent dry weight) cannot be digested by man, seaweeds are considered to be a poor source of energy.

SEA GRASSES

Two genera of seed plants, as opposed to algae, occur abundantly in local marine waters. These are the eel grasses, *Phyllospadix* and *Zostera*. While superficially they appear grasslike, they are not related to true grasses. These perennial, rooted marine plants are thought to have originated in fresh water and subsequently adapted to a marine environment. These plants bloom under water; fertilization is effected by threadlike pollen carried by water rather than air or insects, as is the case in most land plants. *Zostera*, or true eel grass, is dull pale green in color, and has longer, more delicate blades than *Phyllospadix*. It is found growing over mud and sand bottoms in sheltered areas and is a favorite food of sea birds and many other marine animals. *Phyllospadix*, also known as false eel grass, or surf grass, is easily distinguished from *Zostera* by its bright emerald green color, shorter length, 91 centimeters (to 3 feet), and wiry blade. This is a plant of open, exposed waters. Both *Zostera* and *Phyllospadix* have been used to some extent on the Pacific coast for basket weaving.

*Surf grass (*Phyllospadix *sp.*) *is found on rocky coasts exposed to the full force of ocean waves and is the favored habitat of many invertebrates which find a degree of protection within the grass bed. Worms, isopods, many snails, and fish such as the snailfish can be found on the grass blades or near the roots. When in flower, male and female blooms are found on separate plants.*

Pierre Dow

Sponges

"To throw in the sponge," an expression commonly used to admit defeat, had its roots in boxing. At the end of the match, the sponge used to mop the fighters between rounds was thrown to the center of the ring as a token of defeat.

"Sponge cake," "bath sponge," "to be a sponge," "to sponge up liquid," are all well-used words and terms in the English language. They owe their origin to the lowliest of animals, the living sponge.

Sponges are the most primitive of all many-celled animals. Only the single-celled protozoans trail them in development. It is estimated that 4,500 species of sponge are living today, all of which are marine with the exception of one fresh-water family. The fossil record tells of sponges being alive as far back as 600 million years, a half-billion years at least before even the most primitive man appeared on earth. During this great length of time the sponges have changed little; carrying out a most basic life history of living, reproducing and dying.

The sponge is so simple; it is essentially a loose aggregate of cells. The cells are not organized into definite tissues, much less organs, and one wonders why they really bother to stay together. Sponges have no muscle, no nerves, no sensory cells to tell them if it is day or night — not even a mouth.

All sponges are based on essentially the same basic body plan. This is a vaselike structure attached at one end and opened at the other. One layer of plate-like cells covers the exterior of the vase. "Collar cells" line the interior of the vase with a layer of cellular secretion, known as *mesoglea*, sandwiched between the two. The collar cells are like small cups having tiny whiplike tails, known as *flagella*, extending from their centers into the open interior cavity of the sponge. As the flagella beat, water is drawn into the sponge cavity through many minute pores penetrating the sponge's body wall; it exits through the larger opening at the sponge's summit. The water exit is known as the *osculum* and is generally large enough to be seen with the naked eye, while the incurrent pores are too small to be seen clearly.

While still based on the "vase" theme, many sponges have many body cavities and oscula forming an elaborate system of canals. Encrusting sponges, such as the local red varieties, are an excellent illustration of this, with their multiple oscula looking like small volcanoes scattered over the sponge's surface. This kind of sponge may bear little visual resemblance to the vase structure previously described, yet it is functionally the same.

Since the sponge lacks a mouth and digestive tract, it is difficult to imagine how its body cells receive nourishment. In this animal, feeding is accomplished by the collar cells. Minute food particles carried in the water are brought into the sponge cavity where they become entrapped and engulfed by the individual collar cells. Food size is thus predetermined, because only particles small enough to be eaten by a single cell can be used. Digested nutrients are distributed to non-feeding cells by bodies in the mesoglea known as *amoebocytes*. Waste products are simply released from the individual cells and carried away in the constantly circulating water currents.

Amoebocytes not only deliver the groceries, but also produce eggs or sperm for reproduction and secrete a very basic skeleton. The skeleton takes the form of small slivers of glass, calcium or fiber, depending on the species of sponge. *Spicules*, as the slivers are known, give firmness to the sponge and keep it from collapsing on itself and so closing the canals and cavities needed for water circulation.

Because some sponge species can differ greatly in shape, size and color, the size, shape and composition of the spicules is often the only definitive means of identifying many sponges. For example, the local cloud, or trumpet, sponge (*Aphrocallistes vastus*) can be a few inches long in finger-like projections, or it can be huge masses as tall as a man and shaped like a trumpet or a large, soft cloud.

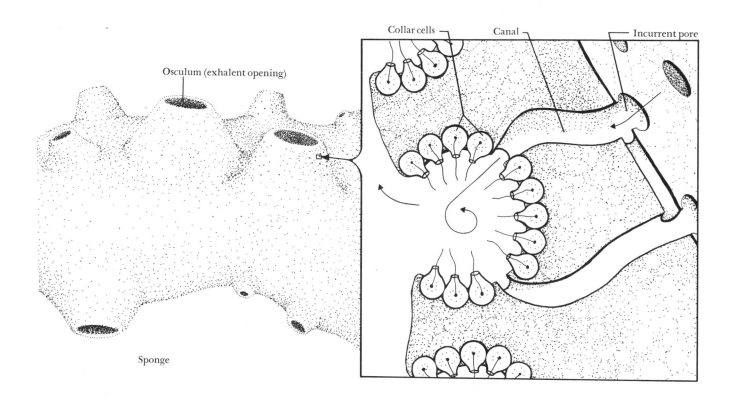

Collar cells — Canal — Incurrent pore

Osculum (exhalent opening)

Sponge

The thin encrusting sheets of sponge bear little resemblance to the huge globular masses of some sponges or the delicate fronds of others. However, some species, particularly those of still waters, do grow to a consistent and recognizable pattern. Among them are such fancifully named sponges as lyre, peacock's tail and Neptune's goblet. The local tennis ball sponge (*Craniella spinosa*) grows consistently to a fuzzy version of its namesake.

Sponges reproduce themselves both sexually and without the fusing of sex cells. Sponges are not male or female, but hermaphroditic, producing both eggs and sperm. The gametes are released at different times to allow for cross-fertilization and are expected to meet by chance as they float about in the sea. After fertilization, the larva floats about for a long time before settling to the ocean bottom, never to move again as it grows into an adult sponge.

As with most lower animals, sponges possess remarkable powers of "regeneration." This is the term given to describe the process of regrowing lost parts. Commercial sponge-growers take advantage of this phenomenon by "planting" pieces of cut-up sponge, much the same as gardeners do with potato slices to produce many potato plants from one tuber. Sponges are also able to regroup their cells if divided. Some species can be strained through fine mesh bolting silk and, given time, the separated sponge cells will re-organize themselves into a complete sponge. No other animal is capable of such total recovery from such extreme mutilation.

Sponges, because they are totally devoid of move-

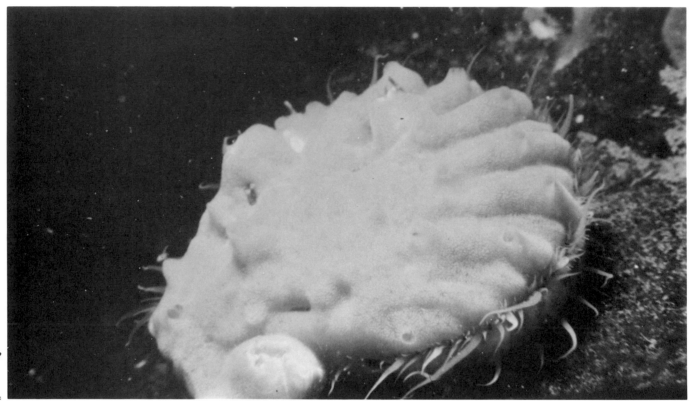

John F. Quail

ment (save the beating of the flagella), cannot walk, crawl or drift away from a deteriorating environment. Instead, some will simply distintegrate to a small blob of cells and wait out the situation, regenerating again in better times.

Belying their apparent innocuous appearance, sponges are not entirely inoffensive. The boring sponges attack the shells of many molluscs (shellfish), eating away chemically at the shell causing it to disintegrate. A local boring sponge, *Cliona celata*, is seen as small yellow patches on the shells of some scallops. Below the shell is the mass of honeycombed sponge. Boring sponges attack non-living mollusc shells as well, and are thought to be substantial contributors to the natural breakdown of shell material littering the ocean floor.

Few animals prey upon sponges. The uninviting texture of sponge tissue, due to the spicules, is very

likely a deterrent, as is the offensive odor of some species, such as the foul sponge (*Lissodendoryx noxiosa*) so named for its foul smell. However, some nudibranchs (sea slugs) and snails persevere and eat sponge anyway. A beautiful little sea slug, *Rostanga pulchra*, has taken on the brilliant red of the encrusting sponge it feeds upon. This encrusting red sponge (*Ophlitasponia pennata*) is seen as red or orange patches on rocks of the lower intertidal level.

The sponge is considered a dead end in terms of evolution. It was an experiment of nature that worked (as can be attested to by its continued presence), but one that did not give rise to a more complex animal. Somewhere near the main stem of the evolutionary tree sponges deviated, and for this reason they are often termed *Parazoa*, meaning "beside the animals," as opposed to the other multi-celled animals known as *Metazoa*.

The sponge Iophon pattersoni.

John F. Quail

Cloud sponge (Aphrocallistes vastus). *Huge masses of cloud sponge occur at depths of 20 m (66 ft.) or more. Because the spicules of this species are composed principally of silica, it is referred to as a glass sponge.*

The convoluted mass of sponge provides shelter and protection from enemies for many fish and invertebrates.

J. Willoughby

In some ways sponges could be considered more interesting dead than alive. Venus' flower basket, for example, is the glass skeleton of a deep water tropical sponge and is frequently displayed in museums. The fiber skeletons of many "spongin" sponges have had innumerable practical uses since historic times. This is known from Greek mythology which refers to Glaucus of Anthedon as a sponge diver. Ancient writings tell of Greek soldiers going off to war with sponge padding in their helmets and leg armor. Wives left behind no doubt used sponges to bathe themselves and their children. In times past, sponges were used in the manner of cups for drinking; Christ was offered a sponge soaked in vinegar.

This "natural" sponge was, and still is to some degree, harvested from tropical waters. The live sponges are fished using trawls, poles or divers. They are then cleaned on the sponge boats or taken to shallow ponds and left for the soft tissues to rot, after which they are squeezed clean in sea water and left to dry. The resulting sponge is the protein skeleton of the once living animal with all cellular tissue removed. No sponges having this particular kind of skeleton are found in the Pacific Northwest, most commercially usable species occurring only in tropical waters.

Today, natural sponge is very expensive and has largely been replaced by synthetic sponges of rubber or plastic. It is worthwhile reflecting on the comfort and convenience provided us by synthetic sponges and note that the inspiration for these came from the skeleton of one of nature's dullest creatures.

Plant or Animal?

Cnidarians . . . Jellyfishes, Anemones, Sea Plumes, Corals and Sea Pens

It is not surprising that for many years the group of animals known as *cnidarians** was considered to be neither plant nor animal but a connecting link between the two kingdoms. These tentacled creatures, often lavishly frilled and beautifully colored, are strongly reminiscent of springtime flowers. Yet the cnidarians are carnivorous animals, albeit primitive in structure.

There would appear to be little similarity between a tiny coral polyp, a sea anemone and a floating jellyfish; yet the animals are closely related. They are based on the same simple body plan of a hollow sac — closed at one end, opened and fringed with tentacles at the other. Imagine a cup with tentacles surrounding its rim. When the cup is securely attached by its base to some firm surface, tentacles and opening directed upwards, it is known as a *polyp*. When the cup is suspended upside down in the water, unattached and free-floating with opening and tentacles on the underside, it is known as a *medusa* or jellyfish. The jellyfish structure has been named medusa for the snaky tresses of the mythological maiden, the Gorgon Medusa.

Many of the cnidarians have both an attached polyp form and a free-swimming medusa form in their complete life cycles. These two distinct forms occur in alternate generations, so that the offspring do not look the least like their parents but are identical with their grandparents. The polyp reproduces a medusa, or jellyfish form, by asexual budding. Unlike the polyp, the medusa offspring are sexually distinct, being either male or female. The eggs or sperm are shed into the water where fertilization takes place. The resulting larvae then settle on an appropriate substrate and develop into an attached polyp generation bringing the life cycle full circle.

As there are over 9,000 species of cnidarians

classed into three major groupings, it can be expected that there will be modifications and short cuts occurring in the life histories of many species. For example, in the primitive fernlike hydroids (Class *Hydrozoa*) the polyp is the dominant generation. In the true jellyfishes (Class *Scyphozoa*) the medusa stage is dominant with a much reduced polyp generation. In the more advanced sea anemone (Class *Anthozoa*) the medusa generation has been completely dropped in favor of the attached polyp form.

Whatever the form, attached or free-floating, the cnidarians are anatomically simple. There is a single opening for taking in food and rejecting indigestible matter. The opening is known as the mouth; the internal cavity as the stomach. There is no circulatory system, no excretory system, no respiratory system. The coelenterate body has only two cell layers forming an inside sheath — the stomach lining — and an outside sheath forming a skin. Consequently, each cell is in direct contact with the water and is able to obtain oxygen and diffuse cellular wastes without complex structures such as kidneys, glands and blood stream.

Between the two cell layers is a cellular secretion known as *mesoglea*. This is the "jelly" of the jellyfish. The mesoglea is much reduced in the polyp forms such as the sea anemone.

Covering the cnidarian body is a nerve network providing the animal with a simple nervous system. As a part of this nervous system there are specialized sensory cells in the medusa form. These are the photo receptors and the statocysts, both located at intervals on the outside margin of the jellyfish bell. The photo receptors or "eye spots" respond to light, causing the jellyfish to be attracted to or repelled by it, as fits the habits of the particular species. The statocysts serve to balance the jellyfish, causing a righting reflex should the jellyfish become disoriented. Because the polyp form is unable to move it has little need for balancing or light organs.

Movement is accomplished in the floating medusa

* previously known as *Coelenterata*

by a rhythmic pulsation of the bell. By contracting the bell around its margin, the water contained within is forced out providing a weak jet propulsion. Pulsations may occur from 15 to 150 per minute, depending on the species and the water temperature. Movement is weak and random at best, as the jellyfish has no way of knowing where it has been or where it is going.

Soft, slow-moving, devoid of sense organs to warn of distant and approaching danger, the cnidarians, particularly the jellyfish, present easy prey for hungry predators. Yet these creatures have survived five to six hundred million years in the world's oceans during which time potential predators have increased greatly in numbers and sophistication. How have they survived?

The cnidarians share a not-so-secret weapon — small stinging cells known as *nematocysts*. These are generously distributed over the body, particularly the tentacles, as oval-shaped capsules containing tiny coiled threads which discharge like small harpoons when stimulated by physical or chemical contact. The stinging cell, which is barbed and poisonous, is just one of eighteen different kinds of nematocysts. There are also entangling nematocysts and sticking ones, all combining forces to ensure the capture of any suitable prey item (small fish, invertebrates, etc.) coming in contact with the tentacles. Animals too large to be paralyzed or killed by the injected toxin would most certainly be stung and thereafter avoid further contact. In this way the stinging cells serve both an offensive and defensive function. Nematocysts are disposable in that once they are used or discharged, they are shed, new ones growing quickly to replace them.

The giant sunfish (*Mola mola*) seems to be insensitive to the nettle cells and is said to feed almost entirely on floating cnidarians. Some nudibranchs have the capacity to ingest the cells without causing them to discharge. Once eaten, the cells migrate to the surface of the nudibranch and resume their protective function in favor of the sea slug.

SEA FIRS AND SEA PLUMES — (HYDROZOA)

The hydroids are primitive cnidarians, often overlooked because of their small size, or mistaken for plant growth; hence their popular name of sea fir (as in fir tree branch) or sea plume.

One may wonder how a cnidarian animal that is supposed to be cup-shaped could possibly look like a fir branch. The branching hydroid, usually only a few centimeters in height, is actually a whole colony of tiny polyps all joined together, sharing a common digestive canal and stiffened by calcium or some other firm material in the mesoglea. Each colony forms a fernlike structure, the individual members having budded asexually from a single polyp. In the hydroids the polyp colony is the dominant generation. A sexual generation of hydroid jellyfish are budded off from the colonial hydroid polyp, but these are generally very small and short-lived. The medusa offspring give rise to another hydroid colony.

The hydroid jellyfish are distinguished from the true jellyfish by the presence of a *velum*, a shelf extending inward from the margin of the bell, and a simple four-chambered stomach. As the medusae are sexual animals they contain gonads (sex glands) often clearly seen through the transparent body as four distinct clusters, or stripes, just above the four chambers of the stomach.

The water jellyfish (*Aequorea aequorea*) is a very common hydroid medusa of the Pacific Northwest during the summer months. Colorless and almost transparent, this 10- to 15-centimeter (4 to 6 in.) medusa is recognized by the sixty to one hundred threadlike canals radiating from the center of the bell. Another common hydroid jellyfish is the cross jelly (*Halistaura cellularia*) having a distinct cross formed by the gonads, giving the cross jelly the appearance of being divided into four equal parts. In this species the bell is shallow and 7.5 to 10 centimeters (3 to 4 inches) across. It is seen from May through to the early fall. Eel grass beds, where the water is quiet and clear, is

J. Willoughby

J. Willoughby

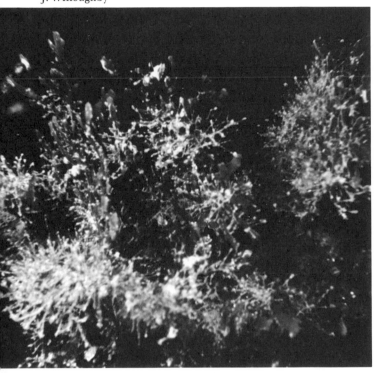

the home of the diminutive 12-millimeter- (½-inch), orange-striped jellyfish (*Gonionemus vertens*), the bright orange color being the gonads. An occasional visitor which blows in from warmer climes is the blue sail or velella jellyfish (*Velella velella*). This species has an erect triangular-shaped functioning sail across the top of the bell.

THE TRUE JELLYFISH (SCYPHOZOA)

In the class of cnidarians known as the *scyphozoa*, the jellyfish generation is by far the dominant one. There are 200 species distributed worldwide and they are distinguished from the hydroid jellyfishes by their large (sometimes enormous) size, their lack of a vellum, and the often elaborate development of oral lobes.

In all medusa or jellyfish the mouth extends from beneath the bell by a short, thick stalk much the same as an umbrella handle. Surrounding the mouth are flaps, liplike structures, known as oral lobes. In the true jellyfishes these lobes are often greatly extended

to form trailing streamers or elaborate ruffles. Some even look like pom-poms hanging on ribbons. These structures are in addition to the tentacles found on the jellyfishes' scalloped perimeter.

The simple four-compartment stomach of the hydroid jellyfish is expanded in the true jellyfish into a complex network of digestive channels. This is most probably an adaptation to the greater size of these animals and the resulting need of a more efficient way to supply more nutrients to a larger body mass. As in the hydroid medusa, the scyphozoan jellyfish are sexually distinct producing in the gonads sperm or eggs which are shed directly into the water. In some true jellyfishes the eggs are retained and brooded in the marginal folds for a period of time before the young strike out on their own. Where a polyp stage occurs (some species skip the polyp stage), the larva settles and develops a polyp in some area sheltered from strong current and wave action. In the true jellyfishes the polyp is very small, about 12 millimeters (½ inch) in

Free-swimming hydroid medusa.

J. Willoughby

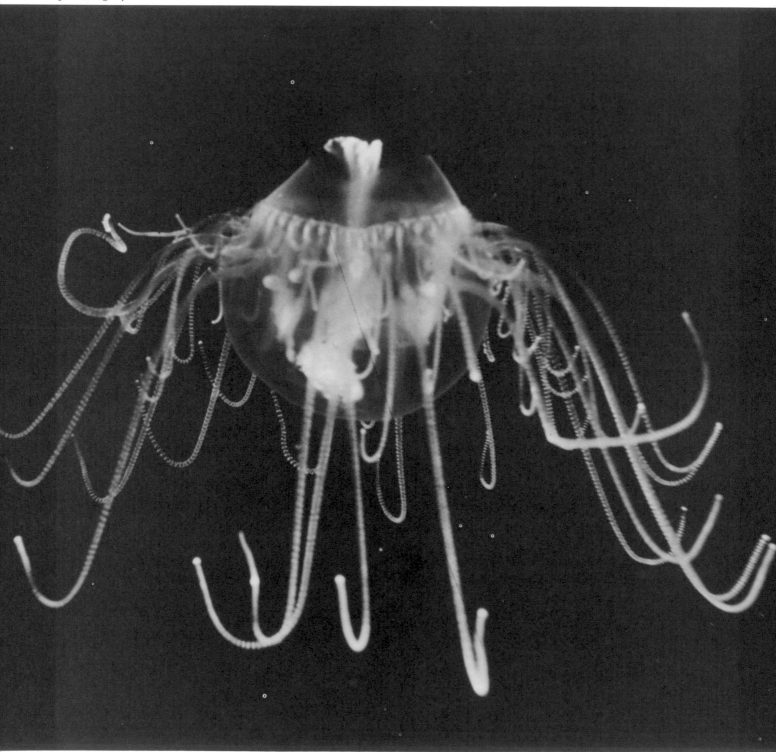

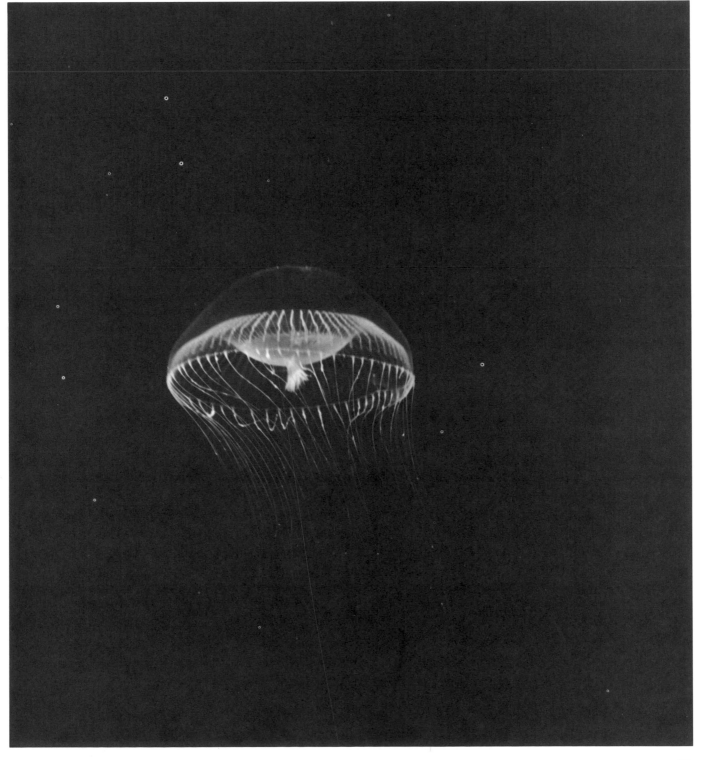

By-the-wind-sailor (Velella velella) is often washed ashore in spring and summer in the Pacific Northwest. It is blown in when brisk winds catch the erect triangular sail.

This species is a highly modified individual hydroid polyp that has taken up life on the open seas. Size averages 5 cm (2 in.).

height, and is never colonial. The polyp elongates into a vase shape and begins to divide crosswise, giving the appearance of a stack of saucers. Each saucer is pinched off as a small jellyfish which swims away and grows to be a big jellyfish.

Just how long this takes, or even how long a jellyfish lives, is not known. It is thought that the complete life cycle, polyp and medusa generations combined, occurs on an annual basis leaving each generation a life span of a few months, the dominant generation living the longest. Whatever the case, in the Pacific Northwest, jellyfish are seldom seen other than in the warmer spring, summer and fall months. One of the most conspicuous of these is the orange-tinted sea blubber (*Cyanea capillata*), a huge (up to 60 centimeters [2 feet] in diameter) jelly mass trailing tentacles of 180 to 240 centimeters (6 to 8 feet) in length. (A North Atlantic relative of the sea blubber is *Cyanea artica*, measuring up to 240 centimeters [8 feet]) across, with tentacles extending 61 meters [200 feet]). The sea blubber is capable of causing a nettle-like sting, even when dead and washed up on shore. Contact with the skin, particularly in children, should be avoided. The moon jelly (*Aurelia aurita*) is a smaller, usually 10-to-15-centimeters (4-to-6-inches) jellyfish common to bays and estuaries. It is colorless except for the four horseshoe-shaped gonads colored violet, pink or yellow. The oral lobes of this species are large while the tentacles are short and delicate.

COMB JELLIES (CTENOPHORA)

Perhaps the beach walker may come upon little oval balls of jelly stranded on the sand looking very much like small jellyfish. These are usually *ctenophores*, or comb jellies, commonly called "cat's eyes" or "sea gooseberries." The comb jellies, though similar in appearance to jellyfish, belong to an entirely different group. They have been included here only because of their similarity to the cnidarian medusa. It must be emphasized that the comb jelly is absolutely unrelated to any cnidarian. They do not pulsate as medusa-type jellyfish do, but are moved through the water by rows of beating hairs, like the teeth of a comb, hence the name "comb" jellies. Where tentacles occur there are only two. These can be extended twenty times the length of the body and are used to capture eggs, larval forms and small fish. There is no alternating of generations.

SEA ANEMONES, CORALS AND SEA PENS (ANTHOZOA)

The *Anthozoa* (the sea anemones, sea pens and corals) have completely foresaken the medusa stage of the hydroids and jellyfishes, retaining only the attached polyp form. They are by far the most conspicuous and successful of the cnidarians with over 6,000 species, 2,000 of which are anemones.

The sea anemones share with some jellyfishes a peaceful beauty and delicacy, an esthetic loveliness of radial symmetry, waving tentacles and colorful hues. It is difficult to believe these simple, almost stationary animals, are carnivorous creatures and, in some cases, capable of doing battle with their own kind.

The sea anemones have improved upon the basic polyp form by having the gut cavity divided into vertical sections by the insertion of membranes known as *septa* which extend from the body wall inward toward the center of the gut. There is a distinct bottom or "pedal disk" in most species which is used to attach the animal firmly to its chosen substrate. The column, or stalk, of the thick body is crowned with tentacles surrounding an "oral disk." The disk has an elastic mouth opening in its center which acts as a kind of permanent lid, closing the end of the tubular body.

Tentacles can number from a few dozen to thousands. Anemones feeding on larger prey such as unwary crabs, invertebrates or small fish, tend to have fewer, stouter and stronger tentacles than those feeding on tiny planktonic organisms. The latter generally have great fluffy masses of very fine threadlike tentacles as seen in local plumose anemones (*Metridium senile*).

The moon jellyfish (Aurelia aurita) may grow to 22.5 cm (9 in.) diameter.

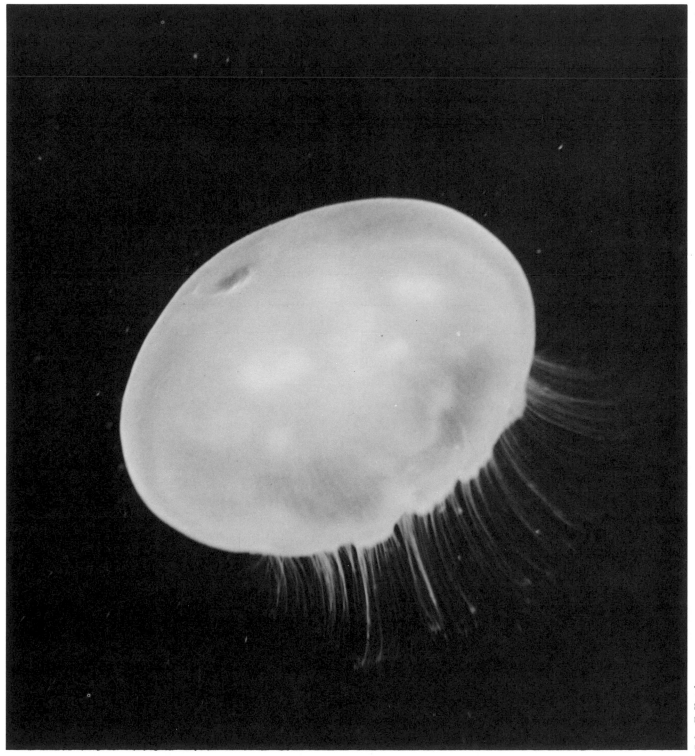

John E. Ketcheson

*The comb jelly (*Pleurobrachia bachei*) grows only to a diameter of 2 cm (¾ in.)*

John E. Ketcheson

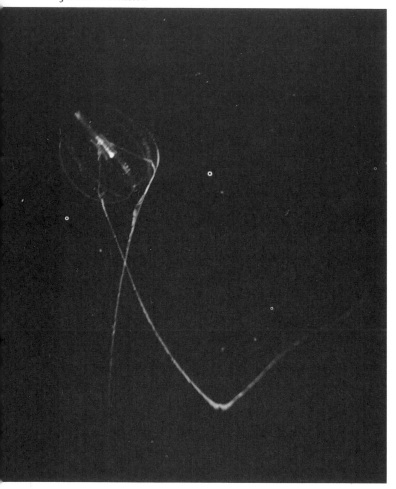

By and large, anemones are not considered mobile creatures though they are able to move very, very slowly by sliding on their pedal disks if environmental conditions indicate a change. This may be in response to a more abundant food supply, a need for greater shelter or less direct sunlight to avoid drying out if exposed at low tide. Statistics indicate that *Condylactis* is the sprinter of the anemone set at 25 centimeters (10 inches) per hour, followed by *Sagartia* at 2.5 centimeters (1 inch) per hour and *Metridium* at 12 millimeters (½ inch) per hour.

Some species of anemone are chauffeured around the sea floor attached to the shells of crabs or molluscs, and one anemone is able to "swim." *Stomphia cocci-nea* is one of the few anemones that will actually flee its enemy, the leather star (*Dermasterias imbricata*). Sensing the presence of a leather star by means of sensory cells on the tentacles and body, the *Stomphia* will release its foothold and by alternate contraction and relaxation of the body column muscles, wriggle away to safety.

Without specialized and efficient locomotory adaptations, the anemones are unable to outrun the majority of potential predators. They have, instead, developed a twofold defense system; stinging cells and size reduction.

Like all other cnidarians, the sea anemone has *nematocysts*, or stinging cells, causing most fish to avoid contact diligently. For predators undaunted by nematocysts, the anemone attempts to reduce temptation by withdrawing its upper body inward, folding its tentacles and oral disk into its body cavity, and thereby reducing itself to an igloo-shaped lump. Some species attach bits of sand and shell to their body columns, further camouflaging their presence when tucked in. Even so, anemones fall prey to a variety of predators: certain molluscs, starfish, flatfishes and some fishes.

Anemones may also fall prey to other anemones, not as food items, but as a result of a territorial action. *Actinia equina*, a wide-ranging and almost ubiquitous species, is able to discourage newcomers which approach too closely. It attacks by inflating small saclike protuberances at the base of the tentacles and leaning over to touch the outsider. Contact with these poison sacs will lead to tissue destruction and death of the interloper if it does not retreat in time.

While effective as a defense mechanism, the nematocysts are primarily a predatory adaptation used in the capture of food. The effect of discharged nematocysts can be felt as a kind of stickiness if the fingers are put into the tentacles of a green surf anemone (*Anthopleura xanthogrammica*). Once prey has been entrapped or stunned by the stinging cells, food items are transferred by the tentacles toward the mouth and into the gut cavity for digestion. Indigestible material is ejected through the same opening.

One of the most intriguing aspects of anemone life history is their reproduction methods. The anemone has not restricted itself to a process of simple pairing but has available a number of reproductive means. Anemones are hermaphroditic, having both male and female gonads; or they are dioecious, having only male or female gonads. The eggs and/or sperm are shed directly into the water through the mouth, tentacle ends, or special pores on the body. Some species even brood their fertilized eggs.

Plumose anemones (*Metridium senile*) are also capable of asexual reproduction. In one such method, the anemone spreads its pedal disk, then draws in the central portion leaving a ring of tissue shreds that have been the perimeter of the anemone's base. Each bit so left develops, or regenerates, into a new anemone. Another method of asexual reproduction is accomplished by a vertical splitting of the animal. A furrow develops on either side of it, running from base to summit. Over a period of hours or days, the furrow deepens until the anemone is split into two complete animals. This kind of reproduction raises some fascinating philosophical problems regarding life and death, at least in anemones. Are the resulting offspring of a split anemone really offspring, or are they duplications of parents? Can this really be considered a new generation? From what point would one begin to calculate the life span of the individual?

Sea anemones are incredibly long-living individuals if we can generalize from the few available documented cases. One of the most famous of these concerns a batch of anemones collected some time prior to 1862 and tended by a lady who changed their water and fed them on fresh liver. Eventually these specimens were given to the Department of Zoology at the University of Edinburgh, where they continued to thrive until they were all found dead in the early

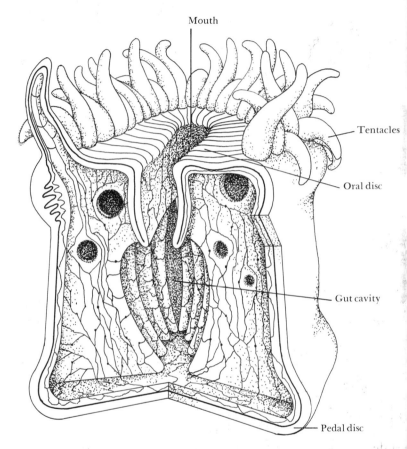

1940s. The cause of death was thought to be human error but, whatever the cause, the anemones were at least eighty years old. Some biologists believe it is possible, and even probable, that anemones could live to at least one hundred or even a few hundred years.

Anemones are also among some of the deepest-living animals, specimens having been dredged from depths of 9,000 meters (30,000 feet) in the Philippine Trench (1952). They also occur high on the intertidal area and withstand the rigors of exposure experienced by all intertidal animals and plants. They have a size range of a fraction of an inch up to 120 centimeters (4 feet) across in the enormous tropical carpet anemones. Locally, the surf anemones are the most abundant

The sea blubber (Cyanea capillata). This jellyfish may grow to at least 60 cm (2 ft.) diameter.

Carnivorous sea anemone (genus Tealia). Anemones of this genus are widely distributed, often very large, with oral disks up to 30 cm (12 in.) across, and occur in a great variety of colors, often with striped patterns. The stout tentacles are a good indication of the genus' ability to feed on relatively large organisms including shrimps and small unwary fishes. ▶

Finn Larsen

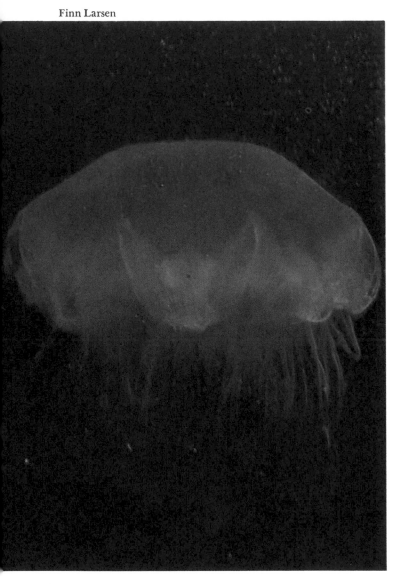

Giant green anemone (Anthopleura xanthogrammica). ▶▶

Another very common intertidal anemone is the 2.5-centimeter (1-inch)-high *Epiactis prolifera.* Though named "small green anemone," it can be either green, red or brown, and can be covered with camouflaging debris.

Large-plumed *Metridium* anemones, up to 30 centimeters (12 inches) in height, have the dense threadlike tentacles of plankton-feeders. Locally, specimens vary from white, orange to dark brown, and are found in very deep waters as well as near the low tide mark. A number of large *Tealia* anemones occur, distinguished by fewer, thicker and stouter tentacles than the fluffy plumose variety. Some are red to pink, with beautiful banding patterns on the tentacles.

SEA PENS

The sea pens, named for their resemblance to the plumed quill pens of old, look and behave as a single organism, yet they are not. The sea pen is a colonial animal and is placed in the same group as anemones and corals. Each "leaf" of the plumed portion of the sea pen has many tentacled feeding polyps on its leading edge. It is the structure and function of the individual polyps which are so closely allied to the polyp form of the anemone and coral. The stalklike body, plumed on its top half, is supported by an internal stiffening rod, allowing the sea pen to stand upright on the sandy bottoms where it lives. The foot end digs into the sand by peristaltic (wormlike) movements, the result of alternate expansion, with water, and contraction. Once buried, the foot end extends itself with water, creating a firm anchorage for the upright sea pen. Sea pens have a reasonable degree of mobility and are able to withdraw their bulbous end, moving on to a more favorable environment if conditions warrant a change.

The local species *Ptilosarcus guerneyi* is approximately 50 centimeters (20 inches) when fully extended and a mere fraction of that when contracted. It ranges in color from pale to deep orange and is found sub-

intertidally on the rocky shores. The smaller of two species (*Anthopleura elegantissima*) occurs in large beds, often in tide pools, while the larger species up to 20 centimeters (8 inches) (*Anthopleura xanthogrammica*) occurs singly and more toward the subtidal region. The deep green color of the latter is due to the presence of a commensal alga growing in the cells of the anemone. If deprived of sunlight for a period of time, the infecting plant dies, rendering the anemone white.

D. Kramer

Pierre Dow

35

Burrowing anemone (Pachycerianthus fimbriatus). Strictly subtidal, this anemone is placed in a different order from most other commonly encountered anemones. A large proportion of the anemone's stalk is beneath the sand surface. This anemone differs from the others illustrated here in having an anus opening at its base, and no pedal disk as such.

▼ *Sea pen (Ptilosarcus gurneyi).*

▼ *Surf anemones (Anthopleura elegantissima) are common intertidally on rocky shores, often in large groups. Individuals grow to 4 or 5 cm (2 in.) in height and are often seen with bits of sand and shell attached to the stalk.*

J. Willoughby

Pierre Dow

The plumose anemone (Metridium senile) occurs in a variety of colors; white, orange, and brown. Some may grow very large and when the stalk is extended be up to 90 cm (1 yd.) tall. Tentacles are numerous, very fine, and worn in a fluted margin. Plumose anemones are particle feeders, capturing tiny waterborne organisms in a mist of tentacles. Plumose anemones are frequently encountered on floats, in the low intertidal and deeper water.

Finn Larsen

Swimming anemone (Stomphia coccinea) *is a circumpolar species living attached to rocks or shells from the intertidal to 200 fathoms. The swimming anemone has a unique response to predators: when one is perceived, the anemone will release its foothold and flee, swimming by alternate lateral contractions of the body wall.*

Sagartid anemone (genus Cribrinopsis).

D. Kramer

tidally over sand and mud bottoms. A heavy slime secretion bears luminescent granules causing the sea pen to glow in the dark. The sea pen is preyed upon by the striped nudibranch (*Armina californica*) and the pink nudibranch (*Tritonia festiva*).

CORALS

Most people are as surprised to find coral in the Pacific Northwest as they are to find eleven species of shark in this area. Both sharks and corals are animals usually associated with warm, tropical seas.

It is true that none of the reef-building corals occur in temperate waters — that is, those kinds responsible for tropical coral reefs. However, at least three species do occur here. Two of these are solitary, stony corals looking like tiny anemones that have secreted

stony cups to sit in. The cup is actually a skeleton. Both species are small, 6 to 12 millimeters ($\frac{1}{4}$ to $\frac{1}{2}$ inch) in size, and range in color from red to orange, or yellow to grey. The orange solitary coral (*Balanophyllia elegans*) may be found in protected areas or under rocks from the low tide level to 46 meters (150 feet).

A beautiful deep water "soft" coral, known as a gorgonian or pink candelabrum coral (*Paragorgia arborea*), forms a colony branching upward from a central stalk, hence the name "candelabrum." In addition to a stony skeleton, the gorgonian coral secretes a woody material giving rigidity to the 45-centimeter (18 in.)-high colony. The pink candelabrum coral is known to certain areas in waters of 60 meters (200 feet) or more.

▼ *Brooding anemone (*Epiactus prolifera*).*

▼ *Solitary coral (*Balanophyllia elegans*).*

Finn Larsen

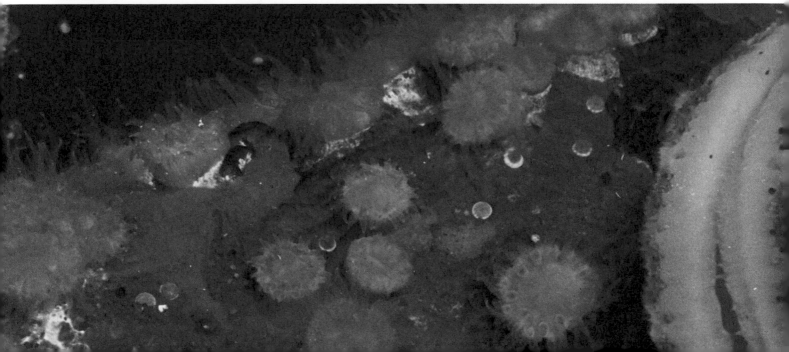

Finn Larsen

Marine Worms

Sand Worms, Plume Worms, Flat Worms, Ribbon Worms and Peanut Worms

Just another rocky beach with bits of seaweed here and there, a few barnacles, and near the tide line some crab casts and broken shells; but turn over a boulder at low tide and there lies exposed a microcosm of marine life. After the crabs and eel-like fishes have beat a frantic escape, look carefully at the underside of the turned boulder. Some small, clear, jelly blobs will perhaps be transparent sea squirts. Some milk-white, sluglike creatures are most likely sea cucumbers, but who or what is responsible for the hard-coiled white tubes firmly glued to the rock's underside? The tube is the home of a small serpulid worm, only one of at least 6,000 living species of marine annelid-type worms.

The name *Annelida* refers to a diversified group of worms. It comes from the word *anellus*, meaning "little ring," and refers to the repeated rings around the worm's body — as in the familiar earthworm. Each ring delineates a segment, the building block of the annelid body plan. Aside from the head and tail segments, all of the body segments, at least in the more primitive annelids, are essentially the same, inside and out. For example, each segment has its own pair of kidneys, and its own nerve exchange site. Like spools, the segments sit on one another and are open in the center to allow for the continuous passage of the digestive tract. Most of the marine annelid worms, unlike the earthworm, have additional structures on each segment in the form of side flaps with bristles. These *parapodia*, as they are known, generally serve two functions: that of movement and respiration. They are, therefore, feet and gills in one.

The fact that the parapodia of some (*polycheate*) worms hang limp and ragged when removed from the sea have earned these worms the name "rag worm." They are more correctly termed *nereid* worms.

A great variety of free-living marine worms of the kind described above can be seen at the seashore — in mussel beds, eel grass or in sand turned up while digging for clams. They can be quite large, up to 60 centimeters (2 feet) long, have beautiful iridescent coloring and a nasty bite. The biting jaws are hidden back in the throat when not in use but can be pushed out and against some likely prey when needed. Nereid worms are active and predatory creatures feeding on other worms, small crabs and shrimps, a variety of larval forms and seaweeds. Nereids make wonderful fish bait and can easily be found in clumps of mussel. The head should be removed before the worm is placed on the hook for obvious reasons.

Nereid worms, for all their fierce and predacious nature, conceal themselves under rocks or in sand for the same reason that makes them excellent bait when fishing. They are attractive food for a great variety of fish as well as some marine mammals and birds.

Among the huge array of polycheate worms a number of species have forsaken the active life of a free-living worm, and its incumbent dangers of predation, for the restriction and security of a fixed life within a protected house of the worm's own making. Hence the worm of the white, coiled house under the rock.

The homes of such worms are known as tubes and the worm within is called a tube worm. There are two common kinds. Those that secrete a limy, hard tube are known as *serpulids* and are generally small. Those that secrete a leathery or parchment tube are named *sabellids* and tend to be larger. One local sabellid (*Eudistylia vancouveri*) builds a tube to 50 centimeters (20 inches) in length with a diameter of 12 millimeters ($\frac{1}{2}$ inch). However, the worm itself, at 15 centimeters (6 inches), is only a fraction of the tube's length.

In assuming a tube-dwelling existence, the tube worms have been required to alter their feeding habits drastically. Unless the worm is able to feed within the security of its home, the benefits of building a house would be greatly diminished, as the worm would have to forage away from the tube and therefore present itself as easy prey. In response to the food

A scale worm (Halosydna brevisetosa).

Nereid worms are nearly everywhere at the seashore. They range in size from small inconspicuous species to the very large ones, in excess of 80 cm (32 in.). As annelid, polychaete worms they are generally easy to distinguish by their segmented bodies and paired bristles or flaps on each segment running in a continuous line down the sides of the worm.

problem, some tube worms have developed beautiful plumed "feathers" at their head ends which they can expose to the water from the tube's open end. Fine hairs on the plumes, covered with mucus, trap floating particles. The mucus and entrapped food is then swept toward the mouth by the beating of the hairs and swallowed. The leathery-tubed worms (*Sabellids*) have particularly branched plumes, much more so than the serpulid worms, resulting in their commonly being called "feather duster" worms. The plumes not only capture food but absorb oxygen as well, thus serving as gills. Eye spots at the base of the feathery structures are very sensitive, so that even a shadow passing over the plumes will cause the worm to withdraw them instantly into the tube. Calcareous tube worms (serpulids) have even developed a "stopper" which is held against the tube's opening once the worm has withdrawn. Should a fish or some other predator be quicker than the "eye" (of the tube worm) and chance to bite off part of the feeding structure, it is not a permanent loss to the tube worm which is quickly able to regenerate, or regrow, such lost parts.

Tube life imposes some additional problems on the tube-dwelling worm. As the tube is closed at its posterior end, the worm must arrange for the elimination of digestive wastes. To this end, a cilia (hair)-lined channel has developed in some which serves to sweep wastes effectively from the worm's posterior end, forward to the tube's open end and out, keeping the tube free of waste material. In the same way, eggs and sperm are released to the open sea to be fertilized by chance. Since tube worms often occur in large aggregations and spawn simultaneously in response to some complex rhythm, much of the chance is eliminated. Even the free-living nereid worms, not restricted by life in a tube, do not copulate but come together in groups at spawning time, releasing eggs or sperm through ruptures in the posterior body segments.

With so many worms inhabiting the marine environment worldwide, from the intertidal zone to waters more than many hundreds of feet in depth, no clear and absolute definition can be drawn between the free-living, nereid worms and their modified cousins, the plume worms. A whole host of forms exhibiting all manner of peculiar modifications occurs in between. For example, the lugworm (*Abarenicola pacifica*) digs a U-shaped burrow but secretes no tube. This worm is responsible for the coiled sand casts found on the sand surface of quiet bays. The casts are the feces resulting from the worms eating their way through the substrate. Another strange worm is the terebellid (*Thelepus crispus*). This animal puts together a soft mud tube but, instead of plumes, it spreads many fine, long tentacles over the sea bottom to collect detritus and particles of food which happen to rest within the tentacles' reach.

Plume worm (Eudistylia vancouveri). *These worms characteristically occur in large clumps of many individuals. When the plumes are exposed the mass looks like a great bouquet of chrysanthemums. Individual plumes can be 5 cm (2 in.) in diameter and are generally colored a deep maroon with green bands. The tubes housing the individual worms may be over a centimeter (½ in.) in diameter and 25 to 60 cm (10 to 24 in.) in length. Rocky, intertidal areas and pilings are the preferred habitat of the species.*

Pierre Dow

FLATWORMS (PLALYHELMINTHES)

All flatworms are not flat; nevertheless, they are so named and certainly those most easily recognized in nooks and crannies at low tide on a rocky beach will inevitably be flat, very flat indeed. So flat are the recognizable intertidal flatworms that they are commonly called "leafy" flatworms for their resemblance to a small leaf in shape and thinness.

Although in this book flatworms have been placed together with other worm forms for the sake of continuity, in terms of evolutionary development, the flatworms belong back near the beginning, following the comb jellies or ctenophores. In terms of physical development, flatworms are not as sophisticated as the segmented worms. For example, flatworms have no specialized respiratory organs or tissues, such as gills, for the absorption of oxygen. There is no circulatory system, such as heart or blood vessels, to distribute nutrients and supplies to the cells. There is not even an anus to dispose of indigestibles which must leave the way they came in, through the mouth. There is typically a mouth, a sac for a stomach, and, surprisingly, complex reproductive equipment of both sexes in each worm, a development which appears out of proportion to that in the rest of the organism. In short, the flatworm is bent on eating and reproducing, and

little else. It is not surprising, then, that two of the three classes of flatworms have evolved a totally parasitic way of life. Examples of such flatworms are the dreaded tapeworms and various internal flukes infesting both man and beast. However, the parasitic flatworms are not to be confused with the free-living polyclad flatworms of the intertidal region.

It is interesting to note that flatworms are considered to be the first group of many-celled animals to show *bilateral symmetry*. This simply means that flatworms are the first of the lower animals to have indications of a distinct right and left side in relation to a distinct front and back; that is, one side is a mirror image to the other. This bilateral (two-sided) symmetry (sameness) is considered an improvement over the radial (round or radiating) symmetry of jellyfishes, anemones and hydroids. This presumably means that the flatworms have advanced over the anemones et al. Polyclad flatworms, so named for their many-branched stomachs (*poly* = many, *klados* = branched), move over rocks, mud or whatever the substrate by gliding on a track of secreted slime using backward sweeps of the cilia which cover the worm's lower surface. When potential prey is recognized, a portion of the pharynx is everted from the flatworm's mouth which is located in the middle of its underside. Descending on its meal like a limp umbrella, the flatworm engulfs small creatures such as other flatworms, tunicates and shrimplike animals. The polyclads are strictly carnivorous, eating only animal material. One small polyclad has been observed feeding on barnacles, which it harasses by crawling up the side of the barnacle's shell and appears to secrete some irritant or poison into the barnacle's interior. The barnacle responds by waving its cirri (tentacles) as if trying to swat an elusive fly. Eventually, the barnacle is overcome and the flatworm dives into the barnacle shell to consume its now moribund tissue.

J. Willoughby

RIBBON WORMS (NEMERTEANS)

Ribbon worms are generally not found crawling around in plain view, though they are certainly common in rocky areas or wherever large numbers of attached animals and plants occur to provide the worms with both cover and food.

Ribbon worms are typically long and thin, and, unlike the annelid worms which show strong segmentation, the ribbon worms are smooth, soft, slender and very elastic. They are fragile creatures which tend to break apart easily if handled. In fact, the ribbon worms give the impression of being not quite "done." They appear to lack all the stuffing they should have, causing them to be slightly flattened or flaccid looking. Their skin is so soft that it seems to have not quite finished toughening and should therefore be pro-

tected in some way. In fact, some ribbon worms do secrete a papery tube about themselves.

A number of ribbon worms are common to the Pacific Northwest. These may range in size from a few centimeters to over 18 meters (60 feet) in length, and range in color from deep blood-red to brown, or combinations of contrasting bellies and backs or bandings of various sorts.

Not only do ribbon worms lack the segmentation and parapodia of the annelid worms, they also lack the biting jaws. Instead, the ribbon worm captures its prey of polycheate worms and small shellfish by using what is called an *eversible proboscis*, which is used in much the same way as a frog's tongue. When the worm shoots out the proboscis, prey is captured by the gluey or barbed end, poisoned to calm its frantic efforts to escape, and then eaten.

43

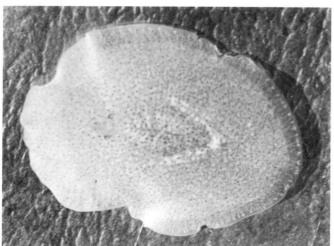

Parchment-type tubes of the feather duster worm (Schizo-branchia insignis) as seen at low tide.

A polyclad flatworm.

The nemertian worm (Amphiporus bimaculatus). The head bears a pair of dark wedge-shaped marks.

A peanut worm (phylum sipuncula).

PEANUT WORMS (SIPUNCULIDS)

Another worm of rocky shores is the peanut worm (*phylum sipuncula*), so named for its resemblance to a shelled peanut when in the contracted state. When extended, the 5-centimeter (2-inch) peanut transforms into a 10-centimeter (4-inch) worm, narrow at the head end, but bulbous at the hind end like a baseball bat.

Peanut worms are found intertidally on rocky shores under rocks or in crevices where sand and mud have become deposited. The drab color of the two most comon local species (*Phascolosoma agassizzi* and *Themiste pyroides*) and their burrowing habits make these worms something of a challenge to locate. A careful sifting of mud out of some protected pocket will generally yield a smooth, leathery, tough peanut worm.

Peanut worms lack the rings or segments of the annelid worms like the bristle or rag worms. They also lack the jaws of the latter. Instead, peanut worms have fine mucus-covered tentacles which are extended out of the mouth when feeding on suspended particles or detritus in the sand and mud.

As an adaptation to living in a burrow, the peanut worm has its anus forward so that it opens approximately one-third the animal's length from the mouth. This allows the worm to eliminate wastes without fouling the burrow or having to turn around. Peanut worms are either male or female but do not mate. Eggs and sperm are shed to the open water where fertilization occurs and results in a small larva. After a period of free living, the larva settles and becomes a regular peanut worm. Whether the peanut worm is as edible as its namesake is questionable.

Moss Animals

Bryozoans

It seems a paradox to describe bryozoans as abundant and obvious seashore animals, when individual bryozoans average only one sixty-fourth to one thirty-second of an inch in size, yet such is the case. In fact, only a few species occur as solitary individuals; most are colonial forms. That is, many, many individuals live connected together in a large mass, each in a separate little shell-like house, resembling a miniature condominium. As colonies, the bryozoans assume such diverse shapes as to defy definition. Some take the form of low bushy mats, looking as unanimal-like as can be imagined. (Because the mats appear more like mats of moss, bryozoans have commonly been termed "moss animals.") Or the colony may resemble a thin, branching, leafless growth a few inches in height. Others mimic the shape of staghorn coral and yet others form circular silvery patches of lacework on the broad blades of brown seaweed. In short, the bryozoans are a near-impossible group to describe, even for the expert. One almost firm rule can be stated, however, and that is that bryozoans are generally attached to something: rocks, wood, other plants or animals. The ever present exception is a tiny bryozoan which lives free among sand grains.

Individual bryozoans bear superficial resemblance to coral polyps or miniature anemones. The body is saclike with a circle of feeding tentacles around the mouth. Rather than one entrance to the stomach, which acts as mouth and anus as in the coral polyp or anemone, the bryozoan has a complete looped digestive tract which opens to a distinct anus located outside the ring of tentacles. A secreted external skeleton-house protects the animal into which it can withdraw completely when disturbed. No circulatory or respiratory system is present and no nettle cells as in the corals. However, some colonial species have individuals bearing whips or jawlike structures on the sides of their houses, presumably to discourage other settling organisms from establishing themselves on top of a colony of bryozoans and, in so doing, smothering it.

If one finds what looks to be a bryozoan, the unidentified discovery could be placed in a dish of clean sea water, and with patience and the aid of a hand lens the observer should watch for the emergence of feeding tentacles to be sure that what is being observed is an animal and not a plant.

*The colonial bryozoan (*Membranipora*).*

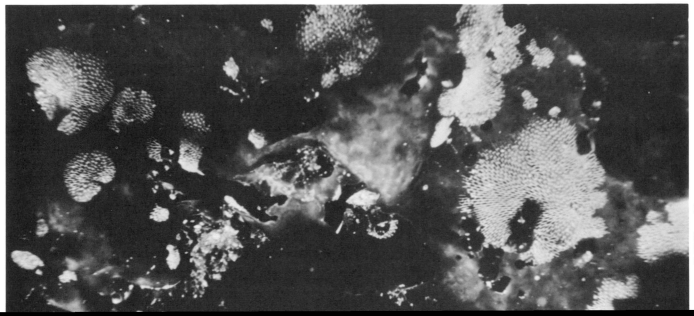

Crustaceans

Crabs, Shrimps, Lobsters and Barnacles

Middaugh

The last time you savored the buttery flesh of fresh crab or shrimp you were actually eating a relative of the common sow bug. Unlikely as it may seem, crabs, shrimps and their marine relatives share an ancient kinship with an enormous group of animals including insects, spiders and centipedes. Collectively these are known as the phyllum *Arthropoda*, meaning "jointed limb."

The marine arthropod branch of this extensive group is known as the *crustacea*, or "crusty ones," and has a membership of over 26,000 — crabs, shrimps, lobsters, barnacles and related forms. While some of these occur on land and in fresh water, the majority make their home in the sea.

CRABS

The higher crustaceans such as crabs can be more easily understood if thought of as a simple body with eighteen pairs of appendages. Unlike the related centipede which has a whole series of identical legs, the crab has adapted pairs of appendages to various functions such as chopping, walking and baby-sitting.

Beginning at the head end, two pairs serve as sensory organs of touch and perhaps smell. These are the antennae and, with the stalked eyes, the balancing organs and the sensory bristles, are the sensory organs of the crab.

Next are a number of modified appendages known as mouth parts, some functioning as knives and forks — cutting, picking and sorting food. Other

46

The edible or dungeness crab (Cancer magister) ranges from California to Alaska from the low tide level to 100 fathoms and is part of an important crab fishery. Legal size for the species is 16.25 cm (6.5 in.) across the carapace. Females mate after molting during the summer in inshore waters carrying up to one million eggs through until hatching the following spring. Large edible crabs may be 25 cm (10 in.). They feed on clams, marine worms and even small fish.

Puget Sound king crab (Lopholithodes mandtii). The brilliant color of the illustrated juvenile will become duller in the adult. This is strictly a subtidal species ranging from Alaska to southern California. When alarmed, the Puget Sound king crab folds its legs under its body becoming a hard stony box. It grows to 30 cm (12 in.).

D. Kramer

mouth parts pulverize and handle food, doing the same job as our teeth and tongues. Food thus prepared is pushed into the jawless mouth passing directly to the stomach where it is further ground by stomach "teeth," much like a food mill. From the stomach, food passes through the intestine where nutrients are absorbed, the unusable "wastes" being excreted through minute openings at the head end and through the anus at the rear.

After the mouth parts, are the most universally recognized appendages, the pincers, or *chelipeds*. One of these is often larger than the other, particularly in males. The function of the pincers is grasping, tearing and defense. To avoid being nipped, it is recommended that a crab be picked up from behind or

from above, across the top of the shell or carapace.

Four pairs of walking legs follow the pincers, operating to move the crab sideways; the legs on one side of the body pulling while those on the opposing side push. Attached to the base of each leg on the underside are the breathing gills.

One would think the appendage supply would by now have been exhausted; not so. The crab can be visualized as a shrimp with its tail tucked permanently beneath itself in a kind of upside-down apron. On the underside of this "apron" are a number of small legs used by the female to hold and brood her eggs. The shape of this uptucked tail is determined by the sex of the crab. In males it is narrow and triangular, while in females it is broad and U-shaped the better to accommodate her large number of eggs.

Many crabs of the Pacific Northwest mate in the fall, with the female holding the male's sperm in a special abdominal receptacle until the eggs are extruded and fertilized. They are held under the tail from late autumn until they hatch and are released in the spring. Like most crustaceans, crabs hatch into a very uncrab-like form — a minute swimming *zoea*. Several molts and some months pass until a miniature crab develops, ready to take up life on the sea bottom or shore.

Growth is accomplished by frequent shedding of the shell. This shell not only keeps the outsides out, the insides in, and is an effective protective armor, but **is** a skeleton too, providing muscle attachment for an animal that has no bones. Once hardened it cannot be added to or expanded. It is a prison and must be dispensed with if the animal is to increase in size. The process of shedding this *exoskeleton* (shell) is known as "molting."

In preparation for the event, hormonal activity stimulates the production of a new, soft, chitinous (*chiton*-tunic) shell beneath the old. When ready, the crab shrinks somewhat and backs out of its old suit through a crack at the waistline, leaving behind every hair and hump including the lining of its stomach with the stomach teeth. While still soft, the crab takes in water expanding the new soft shell to a more desirable dimension, giving an overall increase of 11 to 29 percent, depending on age and, to a lesser degree, the sex of the crustacean. Younger animals show a proportionately greater shell increase per molt than older ones.

The actual molting time (that is, the time taken to shed the old shell) is only about fifteen minutes but renders the newly molted crab vulnerable to predators for at least forty-eight hours before the new cuticle hardens. Some crabs eat the recently molted "cast" in order to supply their bodies quickly with the great amount of lime salts needed to harden the shell. Still,

many casts can be seen on the seashore, so perfectly intact they are often taken for dead crabs. The average number of molts, not counting larval molts, for the Pacific edible crab (*Cancer magister*) is in the neighborhood of fifteen in its life span of five to six years.

While not the same process as molting, crabs are able to part company with their legs or pincers if it is in their best interests to do so; for example, to escape. This is known as *autotomy*. A spasmodic contraction of the muscles near the join between the leg and the body (an area known as a *fracture plane*) releases the limb with a minimum of bleeding. Only blood vessels and nerves, no muscles, pass through this joint. A stub is rapidly formed which, over a series of molts, regenerates a new, functional limb.

Worldwide, crabs exhibit enormous variation in size; from the huge 3.66-meter (12-foot) span of the Japanese spider crab (*Macrocheira kaempferi*) to the minute burrow crabs. They vary equally in habitat, from the tree-climbing coconut and land crabs of the South Pacific to the parasitic and deep water marine forms.

In the Pacific Northwest, crabs are strictly marine, being a large and active army of housekeepers scavenging the shore and sea floor for food. Some are masters of camouflage: the kelp crab (*Pugettia producta*) which so perfectly mimics, in texture and color, the slick olive seaweed where it makes its home; the decorator crab (*Oregonia gracilis*) which masks its presence by securing a collage of plants and animals to its carapace; and the hermit crabs (*genus Pagurus*) which are entirely unrecognized until they move.

The hermit crab should not be assumed to be just any crab that chooses to protect itself further by climbing into an empty mollusc shell, but as a whole separate family of crabs — not quite crabs, yet not quite shrimp nor lobsters either. This "crab" has a soft abdomen, local specimens being flexed to the right in order to accommodate the spiraling of suitable mollusc shells. The tail has become modified to a

Northern kelp crab (Pugettia producta). *Strong and aggressive, this species is most often found clinging to the brown seaweeds it mimics so well in body texture and color. It is generally clean and free of settling organisms. It grows to 10 cm (4 in.) across the carapace.*

Graceful kelp crab (Pugettia gracilis) *inhabits seaweeds and is frequently camouflaged with settling organisms on its carapace. It grows to only 3 cm (1.5 in.) across the carapace.*

Shore crab (Hemigrapsus nudus) *is a very common crab of the intertidal zone of rocky shores. Its carapace is smooth and square, a large individual measuring about 3 cm (1¼ in.) across the back. Coloration in the species is quite remarkable ranging from dark to light, mahogany, green, brown, white and in fascinating combinations. The shore crab is a scavenger and ranges from Alaska to the Gulf of California.*

Pierre Dow

The black-clawed crab (Lophopanopeus bellus) *looks somewhat like the shore crab but is heavier bodied, and has heavier, black-tipped claws. Unlike the shore crab, the black-tipped crab does not generally run when handled but rears up its hind legs and becomes rigid. It is found intertidally under rocks in muddy sand. The carapace measures 2.5 cm (1 in.) across. The species ranges from Alaska to Baja California.*

The porcelain crab (Petrolisthes eriomerus) is a small, flattened crab generally 2 cm (¾ in.) across the carapace. It can be noted that there are only four pairs of walking legs as opposed to the "true" crabs which have five. This indicates that the porcelain crab shares kinship with hermit crabs which also have four pairs of walking legs. (The fifth pair are uptucked and not functional as walking legs.) This species is most common to exposed rocky beaches under loose rocks. It ranges from British Columbia to southern California. The porcelain crab is a filter feeder.

The hairy crab (Acantholithodes hispidus) is frequently taken in crab and prawn traps. It is very definitely a sub-tidal species occurring as deep as 73 fathoms. The hairy crab grows to 10 cm (4 in.) across the carapace and ranges from Monterey, California, to Alaska.

Pierre Dow

Decorator crab without decoration (Oregonia gracilis). Spider-like with small pincers this crab is often so well covered with a luxuriant growth of seaweed and hydroids as to be invisible. The decorator does not simply tolerate and encourage settling organisms but actively decorates itself. When moved into a new environment the decorator will actively redecorate to suit the new environment. The species grows to 5 cm (2 in.) across the carapace and ranges over rocky shores from California to the Bering Sea.

Decorator crab with decoration.

The masking crab (Scyra acutifrons) masks itself with sessile organisms such as sponges, tunicates, and bryozoans. The masking helps camouflage the crab from enemies and potential prey. The carapace is about 3.5 cm long (1½ in.). The masking crab is found on rocky shores from the low intertidal to a depth of 40 fathoms from Alaska to California.

Papilla crab (Phyllolithodes papillosus) is a subtidal species ranging from Alaska to California. The rough textured carapace of the papilla crab blends well with the encrusted rocks of its home. It grows to 5 cm (2 in.) across the carapace.

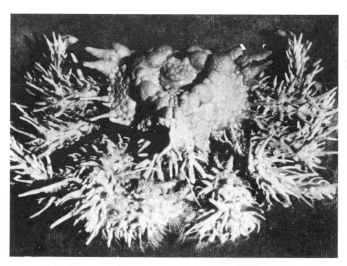

Pierre Dow

Pierre Dow

Box crab (Lopholithodes foraminatus). This slow moving crab depends on its thick and heavy exoskeleton for protection. Like the Puget Sound king crab, when alarmed it becomes a rigid box by folding its legs under. It lives over sand and mud bottoms, feeding on detritus. It grows to 20 cm (8 in.) in width.

Butterfly crab (Cryptolithodes typicus) is so named for the way in which its carapace sweeps out gracefully to the sides like butterfly wings. The species ranges from southern California to Alaska and is infrequently seen on rocks at low tide. It grows to 7.5 cm (3 in.) in width.

hooklike structure for holding onto the "shell house," and the large claws are shaped to block the shell's entrance effectively when the animal is withdrawn. Like other crabs, the hermit crab must molt to grow, and it must find increasingly larger shell houses to complement each new body size. Hermit crabs reproduce in June and July in the Pacific Northwest, the females brooding their eggs in the same manner as other crabs.

Another fascinating little crab that, like the hermit, has surrendered the security of its own hard shell for another approach, is the parasitic pea crab (*Fabia subquadrata*), the female of which is commonly found in the mantle cavity of bivalves such as the Cali-

fornia mussel (*Mytilus Californianus*) and the horse clam (*Tresus capax*). Once established, the crab lives a life of safety and comfort. The male of the species is much smaller and free-living. He pays occasional visits to the female for purposes of reproduction, being small enough to enter and exit between the mussel's shells. Most females become so large and soft they are never able to leave their hosts.

SHRIMPS AND LOBSTERS
No native lobsters occur in the Pacific Northwest north of California and attempts by the federal Ministry of State Fisheries to introduce the Atlantic species

Hermit crab (Pagurus sp.).

*Squat lobster or galatheid crab (**Munida quadrispina**) is a subtidal species ranging from Alaska to Mexico and is frequently caught in commercial shrimp trawls though it is not marketed commercially. It grows to 20 cm (8 in.) in length.*

J. Willoughby

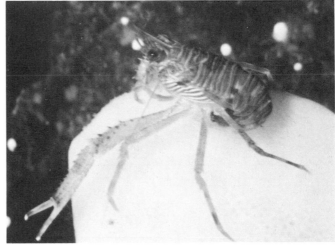

Finn Larsen

John E. Ketcheson

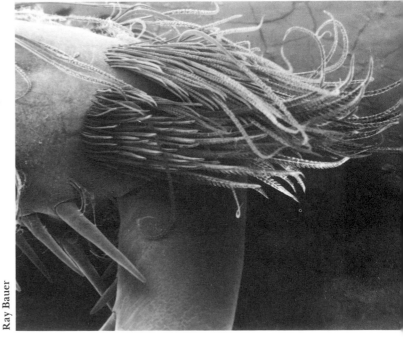

Ray Bauer

*Coon-striped shrimp (**Pandalus danae**). Sand or gravel bottoms where a rapid current exists is the favored habitat of the coon-striped shrimp. A large specimen may be 12.5 cm (5 in.). The species ranges from Alaska to California and is harvested commercially.*

*The last walking leg of the coon-striped shrimp (**Pandalus danae**) magnified 50 times. The grooming brushes (setae) on the legs are used to keep the shrimp's body surfaces and gills free of debris and settling organisms including parasites. It is felt that the ability of the shrimps to "clean" themselves has had much to do with the success of the decapod (ten-legged) crustaceans and their radiation or branching into so many different groups.*

53

Pacific prawn (Pandalus platyceros) *is the largest of the commercial shrimps growing to 22.5 cm (9 in.). It generally occurs over rocky bottoms from Alaska to San Diego, California. Like some other shrimps, it functions first as a male in its second year, changing sex to become female during the third and fourth years. The Pacific prawn is a commercially valuable species.*

Pierre Dow

in British Columbia have been unsuccessful as a commercial proposition. However, some Vancouver-based divers claim a good number of lobsters are alive and well but they are not saying where the potential gourmet dish is.

In contrast to the dearth of lobster is the abundance of shrimp species. Of the eighty identified from British Columbia, six species are harvested commercially for the tail meat. This is the strong muscle used by the shrimp to propel itself backward. By spreading the end of the tail like a Chinese fan and quickly pulling the tail forward the shrimp is able to beat a hasty retreat. Forward movement is achieved by walking or jumping.

Generally, the basic physiology, growth and reproduction in shrimp parallels that of the crabs de-

scribed previously, with one interesting exception. It has been found that the genus *Pandalus* (coon-striped shrimp and prawn) shrimps mature and function first as males, then at two and one-half to three years of age they pass through a transition, or intersexual phase, to become females until their death at four to five years of age.

The shrimp, while perhaps insignificant in size, are of enormous value to the marine community. They constitute a sizable portion of the zooplankton and provide food for many invertebrate organisms: anemones, larval fish, and other marine forms particularly adapted for feeding on zooplankton, such as the baleen whales and the basking shark (*Cetorhinus maximus*).

Many crabs, lobsters and shrimps engage in some

Ghost shrimp (Callianassa sp.) lives in a U-shaped burrow which it digs using its mouth parts, carrying dirt and sand to the burrow's opening with its legs and claws. Food consists of organic material extracted from the mud.

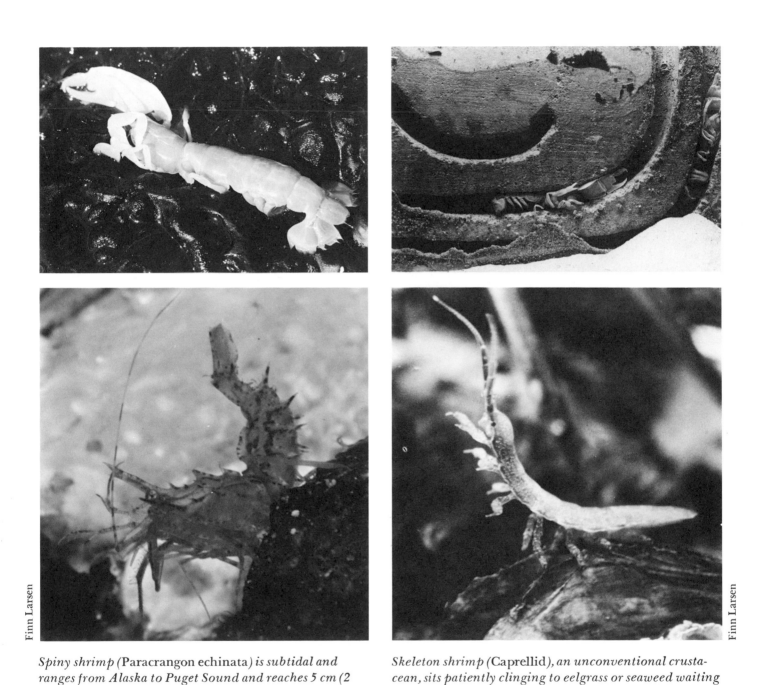

Finn Larsen

Finn Larsen

Spiny shrimp (Paracrangon echinata) is subtidal and ranges from Alaska to Puget Sound and reaches 5 cm (2 in.) in length.

Skeleton shrimp (Caprellid), an unconventional crustacean, sits patiently clinging to eelgrass or seaweed waiting to capture small organisms in its first pair of claws. It grows to 37 mm (1.5 in.).

Isopods. Small buglike crustaceans ranging in size from a few millimeters to 5 cm (a fraction to 2 in.). They cling to rocks, floats and seaweed with claw-tipped legs.

sort of grooming activity. This ranges from a simple scraping in crabs to remove unwanted settlers, to a highly refined process in a group of shrimps known as *carideans*. Antennae, appendages, gills and general body surfaces are brushed and cleaned with special clumps of *setae* (bristles) which form brushes on some of the appendages. It has been established experimentally that if the grooming brushes are removed and the shrimp is, therefore, unable to preen, the animal's gills become so fouled with sediment and detritus that the shrimp dies of asphyxiation. This anti-fouling activity, not just of the gills but of the entire body surface, effectively prevents the settlement of sessile (sedentary) organisms, including parasites. Well-developed grooming behavior is considered as one of the specializations responsible for the initial extensive distribution of the decapod *Crustacea*.

ISOPODS

Many small species of buglike crustaceans occur in the marine environment under rocks, on floats, clinging to seaweed or burrowing in wood. These are known as *isopods*, a term meaning "equal foot." They range in size from a few millimeters to 5 centimeters (a fraction to 2 inches). They have no pinching claws like crabs but generally cling with all eight claw-tipped legs. Over 4,000 different species have been recorded, a number of which are parasitic on other crustaceans such as shrimp, lobsters and crabs. The 2-millimeter common gribbles are responsible for the fine bore holes seen on the surfaces of much beach wood, floats and pilings. Gribble burrows are easily distinguished from those made by the *teredo*, or shipworm (species of burrowing clams), by their much smaller size.

Amphipods. Another large group of small buglike crustaceans with long antennae and the appearance of being hunched over.

AMPHIPODS

Another large group of buglike crustaceans common on wharves, floats, in seaweed and on the beach is the amphipods. The group has in the neighborhood of 3,500 species and includes the beach hoppers and sand fleas. Amphipods are typically flattened from side to side, as opposed to the isopods which are typically flattened from top to bottom. Most amphipods are small, under a centimeter (½ inch), have proportionately long antennae and antennules, and appear to be hunched over.

BARNACLES

Next time you find yourself climbing over rocks near the shore, cursing the plague of barnacles cutting and chewing so painfully at your feet, stop, get down on your hands and knees, and meet this infamous creature eye to eye.

Barnacles are fascinating little animals, incapable of fleeing their enemies. Yet they eat, respire, sense the world around them, and reproduce. In seas the world over 750 kinds are found; at least 23 species in the Pacific Northwest.

There are two basic variations: the gooseneck barnacle and the acorn barnacle. The latter is well-known as a small, firmly attached volcano-shaped structure. Its shell is usually four rigid and fused upright plates with two additional pairs of movable plates at the summit that function as doors, successfully sealing the animal within against the ravages of exposure and predation. The gooseneck barnacle is functionally and anatomically similar but different-looking, having

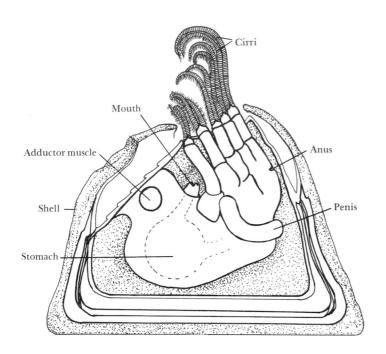

the shelled body attached by a fleshy stalk, or neck, making up two-thirds or more the length of the complete animal. This barnacle, homely in the extreme, looks like a bird's beak on the end of a neck. In fact, stories of birds and barnacles being related abound in old accounts of natural history.

One such account, written in 1597 by the naturalist Gerard, stated that barnacles grew on certain seaside trees in the Orkney Islands, north of Scotland. At maturity, so the narrative continued, the shells would open, giving rise to a species of goose called "barnacles." Infertile barnacles fell to the ground and died. Other similar accounts exist, most probably growing out of a confusion of language and alteration of names. In adition, the Arctic breeding grounds of the barnacle goose were unknown at the time and the "barnacle tree" theory accounted for the existence of progeny otherwise unexplained.

Still later, barnacles were erroneously classified with molluscs, such as clams and snails. It was not until J. Vaughan Thompson in 1830 observed the free-swimming larval form of the barnacle, that it was established as a crustacean in the same company as crabs, lobsters and sand fleas.

The young barnacle is a free-swimming form known as a *nauplius*. At this stage of its life it closely resembles its juvenile crustacean relatives; minute, with a single eye, three pairs of appendages and some means of flotation, usually a drop of oil. This ensures that the tiny animal will float near the water's surface where its food, the phytoplankton, is abundant. The barnacle eats ravenously, growing rapidly and molting every three to five days until seven stages have passed. The juvenile now has a pair of hinged shells and is called a *cypris*. It is this cypris which settles down to the real business of being a barnacle. At only .25

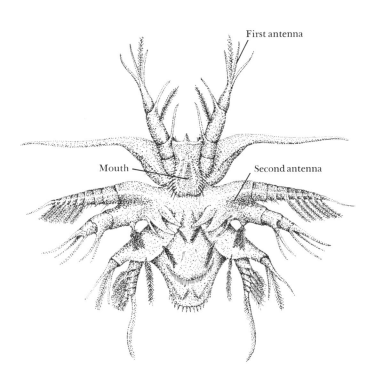

First antenna

Mouth

Second antenna

millimeters (1/100th of an inch) long, it searches for a home site and, once found, glues itself to the spot with a secretion from adhesive glands found near the head. Other glands ooze shell-building material and in no time it has begun to look and behave like an adult barnacle.

Since the barnacle is to be sedentary for the rest of its life, from one to seven years, it no longer requires its six pairs of legs for walking, so instead of discarding them, they are brought into service as food-catchers. The curled, feathery legs extend through the open plates at the barnacle's summit and begin sweeping the water for particles of food — plankton and detritus. Other appendages near the mouth bundle the entrapped food and convey it to the mouth where it passes to the stomach for digestion. This peculiar feeding mechanism led Huxley to describe the barnacle as "a crustacean fixed by its head kicking food into its mouth with its legs."

The barnacle is without a true heart or blood vessels, so nutrients from digested food, and oxygen absorbed from the water, are distributed to muscles and various organs by fluid flowing through passages between them, a simple but efficient method of circulation known as *lacunar circulation.*

But what of growth? How can an imprisoned animal become larger? For the barnacle this means partial replacement of the shell. It is now thought that the exterior plates grow and are added to, whereas the internal support is shed as a new shell, developing beneath, is expanded with water to allow for greater size. It then hardens rapidly. Molts can be very rapid, only days apart, depending upon species, temperature, food and breeding cycles. Whole beds of barnacles may molt simultaneously.

Barnacles may also breed simultaneously with a reproductive potential that is awe-inspiring. A mile of shore can have more than one and a half billion barnacles bringing forth fifteen hundred billion potential young! Barnacles are hermaphrodites, having both male and female sex organs, but they usually do not fertilize their own eggs. Fertilization is achieved, in at least some species, by means of a long extensile penis which transfers sperm to the mantle cavity of a neighboring barnacle. After fertilization the many thousands of eggs are brooded for perhaps two weeks before the hatched larvae are released. It is small wonder, then, that a ship can become heavily fouled with barnacles in as little as eight months. On a large ship this fouling can amount to tons of additional weight, a drastic reduction in speed, with proportional increases in fuel consumption and maintenance costs. Since at least the fifth century B.C. (when the first records of this problem were written) sea-going man has been trying to frustrate the settling attempts of barnacles. In modern times, toxic paint, copper sheathing, chlorine gas, radioactive paint, heat and electric

Thatched barnacle (Balanus cariosus) *is 3.75 to 6.25 cm (1½ to 2½ in.) and is recognized by its steep-walled, thatched appearance. It is found in the surf zone away from fresh-water outfalls. Like other barnacles it is preyed upon by starfish, some birds and perhaps crabs.*

Gooseneck barnacle (Polliceps polymerus). *Where a number of this species occurs, all will be oriented in the same direction so that, as waves fall back off the rocks, the spread feeding cirri of the barnacle will capture floating organisms and small animals. Individuals of this species grow to 25 cm (10 in.) and occur near the mid to low tide level on exposed coasts in the Pacific Northwest.*

impulses have been tried. Yet researchers continue to explore the effects of toxins on barnacles in an effort to find a lasting solution to this expensive problem.

Other researchers are looking to the barnacle for other reasons. Fossil barnacles that attached themselves to shells 15 to 20 million years ago are still attached, a testimony to their adhesive capacity. What fantastic potential there is in this substance that lasts 15 million years; provides a sheer strength of 454 kilograms per 6.45 square centimeters (1,000 pounds per square inch); will bond tissue and bone; can be heated to 177° C. (662° F.) and not melt; or frozen to −146° C. (−383° F.) and not crack or peel; and is not attacked by acids, alkalines or organic solvents. The applications that a successful synthesis of this barnacle glue can give to industry, medicine and dentistry are endless.

A FASCINATING VARIATION
Coronula, the whale barnacle, is one of a few species which attaches itself to the skin of certain whales. Another is said to grow only on the tongue of a particular

turtle. But the worst freeloaders of all are *sacculinids*, truly parasitic barnacles, unlike the former which are simply inconveniences. These sacculinid species are fairly common on a number of local crabs. The larval *Sacculina* reaches its victim while in the free-swimming stage, attaching itself to one of the hollow bristles on the crab's exoskeleton. The bristle is pierced and a few parasitic barnacle cells are released into the body of the crab. These cells come to rest at the junction of the stomach and intestine where they grow, extending rootlike processes throughout the crab's body. The *Sacculina* barnacle now feeds on the crab, destroying its reproductive organs and altering the crab's sex hormones so that, regardless of previous sex, it molts to become a female complete with an apron-like abdomen. During the molt, the parasite is not shed but remains, extending a saclike mass through the abdomen to the outside, while the host's shell is still soft. The sac contains the self-fertilized eggs of the *Sacculina* which are soon released to become more parasitic barnacles. Parasitism by a *Sacculina* barnacle does not necessarily spell the end for a victimized crab.

Molluscs

Snails, Nudibranchs, Bivalves, Chitons, Teredos, Octopus and Squid

The molluscs initially provided food, then tools, and, with time, ornaments and currency. They were abundant, accessible, and often of exquisite beauty. Since prehistory mankind has eaten, used, and even worshipped the shelled creatures.

This animal group is of such spectacular diversity that there would seem to be no beginning and no end. How else does one describe a group of living forms which counts among its kin the garden slug, the shipworm, the clam, snail, abalone, and octopus? All are molluscs and they number some 130,000 living species with many more fossil forms, their history dating back at least 600 million years.

The molluscs have invaded every habitat short of taking to the air. At depths where hydrostatic (liquid) pressure measures 600 kilograms per square centimeter (4 tons per square inch); into the snow-capped Himalayas; on the desert; in fresh, salt and brackish water; some molluscan species will be found.

On the basis of shared characteristics and similarities, the grand group of molluscs has been broken into nine smaller classes. The commonest of these are: (1) the *Amphineura (Polyplacophora)*, having eight shells, as in the chitons; (2) the *Scaphopoda*, having long, tubular shells, as in the tusk shells; (3) the *Pelecypoda*, having two, usually equal, shells as in the clams; (4) the *Gastropoda*, having one shell, as in the snail, or none, as in the slug; (5) the *Cephalopoda*, having tentacles and a shell, as in the nautilus, or having no shell, as in the octopus; and (6) the *Monoplacophora*. The latter was previously thought to have been extinct for 450 million years until a living specimen was dredged from a deep trough off the coast of Costa Rica and described in 1957.

All molluscans, though fantastically diverse in habit, form, size and habitat, share among themselves, and with no other animal group, two characteristics. These are the mantle and the *radula*, though not all molluscs have the latter. The mantle is a fold of soft flesh enclosing the gut, or viscera, and is responsible for secreting a calcareous (calcium) shell. The radula is a toothed tongue. Any other generalized statement regarding molluscs would demand qualification. Therefore, information of a more specific nature will be provided as each molluscan group is described in the following sections.

All classes, except the Monoplacophora, have representative species in the Pacific Northwest. The area claims to have in excess of 900 marine shells. This figure, of course, excludes the non-shell-bearing marine molluscs such as the nudibranch and octopus.

In conclusion, it must be remembered that the shell, while invaluable for identification, is not an animal. It is housing and protection; the animal lives within. Scientists studying molluscs recognize this vital difference and label themselves accordingly: a *malacologist* deals with the animal (soft parts), a *conchologist* deals with the shell (hard parts).

The authors invite you to become both. An excellent place to start is on the beach. Examine the bits of shell and debris left at the drift line for clues to which living molluscs may be found there.

THE SNAILS, NUDIBRANCHS (GASTROPODS)

Have you ever wondered why a snail's shell is coiled? No? Imagine yourself a snail, then, carrying your house on your back, not casting off and growing new shells as you grow, but adding to the one you were born with. With time and growth the shell would gain in height and breadth to accommodate a larger body. The shell would become higher and higher and soon begin to topple and fall. Your house would no longer be an asset but a liability. Consider how much more practical it would be if the house turned in on itself in a low spiral creating an expandable, yet compact and portable abode.

All modern snails and their relations, including snails and slugs both aquatic and terrestrial, are collectively known as *gastropods*. All have a spiraled

*Shield limpet (*Collisella pelta*) has a variable exterior. It may be strongly ribbed or smooth. It grows to 4 cm (1½ in.) in diameter on rocks of the intertidal zone from Alaska to Mexico.*

*Keyhole limpet (*Diodora aspera*) has the same Chinese-hat shape as a regular limpet and, in addition, an opening at its summit. This species is found intertidally from Alaska to northern Baja California, and grows to 5 cm (2 in.).*

shell, at least at their beginning, even if the spiraling may not be obvious, as in the Chinese hat snails and the limpets, or if the shell is reduced or missing altogether, as in the slugs.

Where present, the shell is carried on the snail's back. The top of the spiral, or *apex*, is usually directed to the hind end of the animal with the shell opening, or *aperture* directed to the creature's back, and is held there by the insertion of a strong muscle into the *columnella*, or central axis of the shell. In addition to the large body of the main shell, there may be an *operculum*, or door plate, on the rear top of the snail's foot and this is held against the aperture when the animal withdraws into the privacy, security and protection of its shell. Less highly evolved snails, such as the abalone and limpet, have no operculum and must rely on the tenacity of their grip for protection. As it is estimated that the abalone may exert a suction equal to 4,000 times its own weight, this would seem to be a good alternative.

Gastropods, also known as *univalves*, meaning "one shell," are only one branch of the huge mollusc group which includes chitons, clams and octopus. The gastropods themselves have become so incredibly

diverse, not only in appearance, but in size, habits and habitat. This great diversity has resulted in many fascinating adaptations to the various environments they inhabit and the food sources they exploit. Consequently, few generalizations apply to all gastropods. For the sake of clarity and order the three main camps of gastropods will be briefly described, because in the vast realm of living things familiarity breeds not contempt but understanding.

Terrestrial and fresh-water snails and slugs (with a few marine forms of the high intertidal) are termed *pulmonates* meaning "lunged." The mantle cavity in this group has been modified to function as a lung in order to breathe air. The pulmonates will not be considered further in this description of gastropods.

Most marine snails are separated into two groups according to the location of the gills. Yes, snails have gills tucked away in a pouch known as the mantle cavity. One group is the *Prosobranchia*, meaning "gills in front," and includes nearly all the shell-bearing snails. The other group is the *Opisthobranchia*, meaning "gills in back," and includes the sea slugs and nudibranchs.

It is generally assumed that gills or any other

Abalone (Haliotis kamtschatkana). At least 70 species of abalone occur worldwide. The northern abalone occurs from Alaska to Point Conception, from the low intertidal to 18 m (60 ft.) in depth. Abalone are grazers feeding on algae and diatoms encrusting the rocks where they live, and are distinguished by a row of holes along one side of the large, flat, ear-shaped shell. The northern abalone grows to 15 cm (6 in.) in length.

Abalone are taken commercially for the restaurant and supermarket trade and are subject to size and bag limits in British Columbia. Individual animals must be greater than 6.25 cm (2½ in.) across the shortest diameter of the shell.

In the waters between Vancouver Island and the mainland or in Pacific Rim National Park the daily bag limit is twelve. No abalone may be taken within a mile of Mitlenatch Island in the Strait of Georgia.

Pierre Dow

breathing apparatus will naturally be located in or around the head region. This is true for higher animals, but not necessarily for some of the lower animals. The old and distant ancestors of the gastropods had an arrangement where the mantle cavity housing the gills, anus and genital opening was directed to the rear. Then came torsion, a twisting of the animal's whole upper torso by 180 degrees, bringing the mantle cavity, complete with anus and gills, to lie at the back of the head. Why this strange twisting, unique to gastropods, took place is still a matter of conjecture. One theory maintains that it was the result of a mutation of the side muscles which caused the body to become twisted, the muscles of one side overpowering those of the other. Such an arrangement would be beneficial to the animal for a number of reasons. Most important, it would make easier the work of the tiny hairs, or cilia, which beat constantly in order to maintain a flow of water into the mantle cavity and so to flush the oxygen-hungry gills. When the gills and mantle cavity are positioned at the rear of the animal, the cilia are competing with water currents being directed away from the back of the animal as it moves forward. By twisting the mantle cavity and gills around to the front of the animal, a good current is almost naturally sustained by the creature's movement and by the fact that most animals orient themselves facing into any natural current.

Whatever the reason, the result of torsion is a snail with its stomach in a knot. Torsion occurs very early in the development of young gastropods, within hours of the larvae being fertilized. It must be remembered that torsion is quite distinct from the coiling of the shell and should not be confused with it.

Torsion explains why the marine univalves called prosobranchs have gills in the front, but what, then, explains the opisthobranchs with gills in the back? The latter did not continue to twist and complete the circle but chose to untwist at some early stage of development and go straight.

Interestingly, to twist or not to twist appears to be more or less directly linked to the gender of gastropods. Those which undergo torsion and retain its effects (*Prosobranchia*) are separate sexually, being either male or female. Those which undo the effects of torsion (opisthobranchs such as nudibranchs) are usually forever doomed to hermaphroditism.

Gastropods are so named because they seem to creep on their bellies. The name is derived from the Greek *gaster*, "stomach," and *podos*, "foot." Generally, a sheet of mucus is secreted by the fore portion of the foot so that the snail glides along on its own slime using rippling muscle waves of the foot's inner sole. In some gastropods the foot is modified to float on a bed of tiny moving hairs. In others, such as the local chink shell (*Lacuna variegata*), halves of the foot are used alternately to move in much the same manner as a man would if his ankles were tied together. The result is a "waddling snail." Still other gastropods have extended the sides of the foot into winglike flaps for swimming, like the bubble shell (*Haminoea virescens*).

Gastropods must be able to move about, however slowly, in order to eat, with the notable exception of

Dogwinkle (Thais emarginata) grows to 2.5 cm (1 in.) and is common to rocky shores. It ranges from Mexico to Alaska and has a wide color range. The dogwinkle feeds on barnacles.

Dire welk (Searlesia dira) is a common snail of the rocky intertidal and deeper waters. It grows to 3.75 cm (1½ in.) and ranges from Alaska to California. The species is carnivorous and a scavenger.

Thais snail (Thais lamellosa) has a very variable shell. Sculpturing ranges from smooth to very wrinkled, color ranges from white to orange-brown with a great variety of striping. The Thais are carnivorous snails feeding on ascidians, clams, oysters and barnacles.

This species grows to 3 to 7.5 cm (1¼ to 3 in.) and ranges from California to Alaska from the intertidal to 120 m (400 ft.).

"Sea oats," eggs of the snail Thais lamellosa.

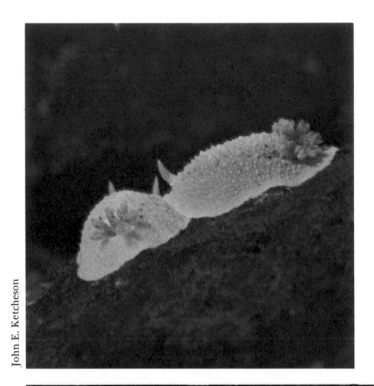

John E. Ketcheson

Sea lemon (Archidoris montereyensis) is commonly found intertidally in rocky areas, in tide pools or near floats throughout its range from Vancouver Island to southern California. Five centimeters (2 in.) is the average length of this species, yet it may grow larger. Black peppering on a yellow ground and on the tubercles distinguishes the sea lemon from other nudibranchs. The plumed gills indicate the rear of the nudibranch, while the stubby, paired tentacles (rhinophores) are at the head end. This species feeds on sponges.

Orange and white nudibranch (Triopha carpenteri). A large white, sausage-shaped nudibranch with orange highlights on raised projections makes this species one of the most attractive found locally. Triopha grows to 12 cm (5 in.) and feeds on bryozoans and small colonial animals associated with a substrate of some kind.

J. Willoughby

Coryphella rufibranchialis. *Nudibranchs generally take one of two shapes. This species is the "aeolid" shape with a long tapering body, and rhinophores which cannot be retracted. Rather than gills, extensions of the body surface known as "cerata" perform the necessary respiratory exchange. This nudibranch is found from the intertidal zone to 300 m (1,000 ft.). It grows to 3.5 cm (1½ in.), eats hydroids, and is thought to live only a year.*

*Opalescent nudibranch (*Hermissenda crassicornis*) is the most nearly ubiquitous nudibranch of the Pacific Northwest and can be found in eelgrass beds or in the rocky intertidal zone searching for its food: hydroids, tunicates, molluscs, eggs of various kinds and even bits of fish. Rather than plumed gills, the* Hermissenda *has many cerata on its back surface which serve the same purpose. The species ranges from British Columbia to California and grows to 5 cm (2 in.) in length.*

J. Willoughby

Martin Roberts

▲
*Periwinkles (*Littorina *sp.) inhabit the upper intertidal zone, often in tremendous numbers, where they graze on film growing on the rocks, or even on the rocks themselves. Local species are seldom larger than 1 to 2 cm (½ to ¾ in.) in length.*

*A snail of the high intertidal zone (*Batillaria zonalis*), this species was introduced with oyster spat from Japan. It grows to 2.5 cm (1 in.) and prefers mud and sand areas.*

the sessile snails (*Vermetidae*) which are suspension feeders. Unlike the filter-feeding clams and oysters which bring in bits of food in the natural course of respiration, the gastropods must seek out their sustenance, be they grazing, herbivorous, scavengers, or deliberate predators. Whatever the food preference, the gathering device is generally the same — the radula. Best described as a long, tooth-bearing tongue, the redula is held in the tubular snout, or proboscis, when not extended and being used for scraping algae or flesh, as the case may be. Salivary and digestive glands act upon the ingested food as it passes through the digestive tract. Unusable products are eliminated via the anus into the mantle cavity which is just above the head in most marine snails.

The majority of marine snails are grazers or nibblers, eating whatever plants and small animals that can be scraped from the rocks. Others are scavengers, eating bits of detritus and dead organisms, and in so doing they fulfill a most important function — a combination of housekeepers and recyclers. Periwinkles, or *littorines*, are very common little snails of the Pacific Northwest intertidal areas, and have reached the ultimate in recycling by actually feeding on organic matter contained in Eocene and Cretaceous silt stone as they rasp and scrape the encrusted rocks. It has been calculated that in 2.6 square kilometers (1 square mile)

of beach in La Jolla, California, there may be 860 million littorines eroding 2,260 tons of this stone in a year. The stone could contain 5,712 tons of organic matter, 6.82 tons of which could be incorporated into the tissues of the living periwinkles.

Other snails are not content to scrape algae slime or eat food a hundred million years old, but must have their victuals absolutely fresh. Bulbous moon snails (*Polinices lewisii*) plow through sand and mud, stalking defenseless clams; *Thais* snails creep with singular purpose over barnacle beds dispatching them as they go; and oyster drills attack the succulent young oysters.

There would seem to be no contest in such a chase, when one considers how difficult it is to part the shells of a clam or oyster which chooses not to have its shell parted. What chance has a mere handless snail? Carnivorous snails make no attempt to compete with the tremendously strong adductor muscles of the bivalves which keep the shelled prey closed; instead, the predators break through the defense of their victims using a combination of a shell-softening secretion and a drilling radula. By alternately softening the shell and scraping it away, a process which may take many hours, the snail eventually gains entrance to the shell's interior. The proboscis then sucks out the flesh and dinner is served. Whether rasping rock, shell, algae or whatever, the radular teeth become worn down. When

Ron Long

this happens new ones grow to replace those no longer functional.

Precise drill holes are frequently seen on the umbo (hinge) region of clam shells cast up on a sandy beach, clear indication that moon snails are about, plowing under the sand.

A pair or two of sensory tentacles, a pair of stalked eyes, and a number of assorted sensory cells provide the gastropod with information about its environment. Depending upon the species, the eyes may be sophisticated organs having a lens and retina. However, most sensory messages received will be chemical ones; subtle changes in the composition of the water around the snail. An example of the efficiency of this system is demonstrated by the fact that an oyster drill will choose a young, still growing oyster, over a mature oyster on the basis of metabolites specific to shell production secreted by the younger oyster.

The animals' chemoreceptors (sensory organs) must, of necessity, play an important role in finding a mate of the opposite sex and of like species in a crowded underwater world. Vision is the least useful for this purpose, since most snails do not possess eyes of sufficient complexity to recognize a mate.

Unlike the bivalves, most gastropods do not release eggs and sperm directly to the water to meet by chance, but mate and copulate. The male passes his sperm to the female via a penis located just behind and beside the head. Eggs are then laid by the female in separate gelatinous capsules with a number of larvae per capsule, as the eggs of the Oregon triton (*Fusitriton oregonensis*). The capsules are commonly referred to as "sea corn." Other marine snails and nudibranchs lay their eggs in a great variety of strings, coils and threads, the temporary cradles of their progeny.

An unusual and frequently seen egg mass is the sand collar of the moon snail. The rubber-like collar does not encircle the moon snail's eggs like a nest, as one would think, but contains the eggs within the solidified sand-and-mucus collar itself. As the larvae develop, the collar begins to disintegrate releasing the juvenile snails.

Contrasting sharply with the heavily laden and ponderous shelled snail, creeping its way among skittering crabs and swiftly moving fishes, is the graceful elegance of the gliding nudibranch. The richness of the nudibranch's color and ornamentation would appear to preclude this animal from being referred to as a sea slug, yet the name is commonly applied in acknowledgment of the nudibranch being the marine equivalent of a land slug. Both animals are considered true snails though they do not sport shells, the larval shell being completely discarded by the nudibranch,

69

Giant nudibranch (genus Dendronotus*). Nudibranchs of this genus are highly variable in color and may be white, orange and spotted. A small species occurs in shallow water, while deeper water often harbors specimens up to 20 cm (8 in.) in length.* Dendronotus *are distinguished by their many-branched cerata which arise from the back of the body like spots of flame. It is generally accepted that the genus feeds on hydroids. There are at least seven species of* Dendronotus *in the Pacific Northwest.*

John E. Ketcheson

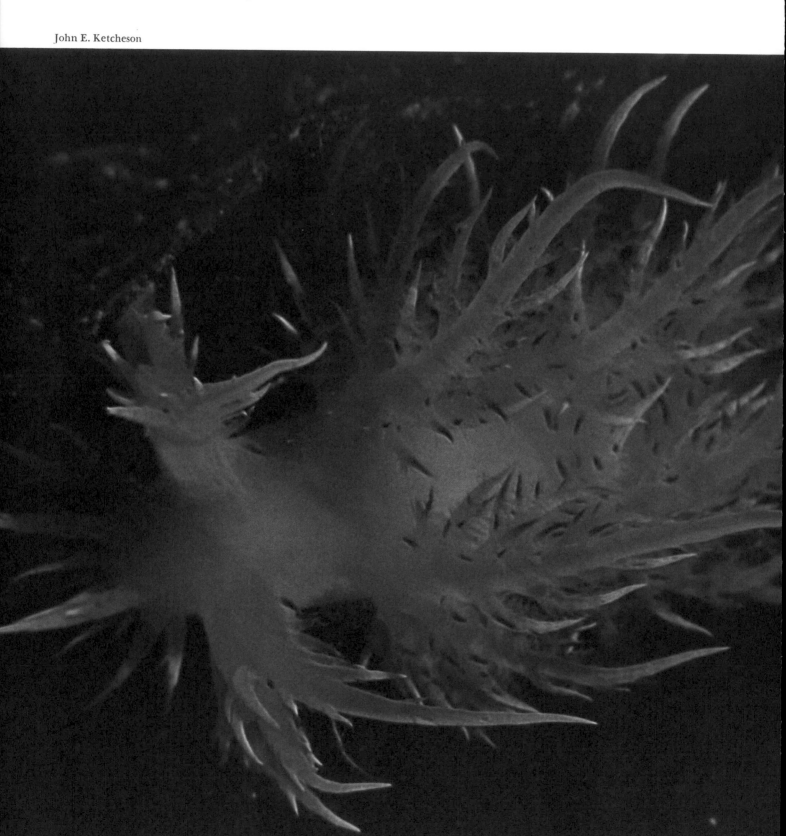

Mossy nudibranch (Aeolidia papillosa), looking like a shaggy brown duster, is widely distributed in a variety of habitats throughout the rocky intertidal zone and on floats. It appears to feed exclusively on sea anemones. The nematocysts of the anemone are ingested and transferred, unexploded, to the cerata of the nudibranch where they become a protective device, a kind of second-hand weapon.

John E. Ketcheson

The olive snail (Olivella biplicata), *looking much like its namesake, and about the same size as the olive fruit, is distinguished by a glossy and smooth exterior. This creature lives just below the sand intertidally from Alaska to California. The olive snail is a carnivorous scavenger. As the olive snail plows through the sand its siphon sticks up, like a snorkel.*

but retained internally in the land slug as a small memento of its beginnings.

Nudibranchs, for all their apparent lack of any protective mechanism, are the forbidden fruit of many potential predators, looking delectable and tasting quite awful. Almost nothing will eat them and they are left in peace to graze on coelenterates and hydroids. At least one, the diaphanous-hooded nudibranch (*Melibe leonina*), uses its large umbrella-like hood, fringed around its edges with feather-fine tentacles, to scoop suspended food particles from the water. If there is no current to deliver food into the hood, the nudibranch throws its hood over prospective food items and closes over them in the same manner as a South Sea Islander uses a cast net to capture fish.

BIVALVES

Single-shelled molluscs have great esthetic appeal in the perfect spiral of their often elaborate shells. The appeal of the two-shelled molluscs is largely gastronomic. No other food quite compares with the delicate flavor and smooth boneless texture of a fresh, raw oyster seasoned with a drop of lemon and a dash of pepper. The eighteenth-century wit who claimed "the man that will eat an oyster, will eat anything," surely based his assumption on the questionable beauty of this creature when divested of its shelly fortress, rather than on the delightful flavor of the animal's flesh.

Oysters, in company with clams, mussels and scallops, form a group of some 20,000 species. A few occur in fresh water, the majority live in the sea, and none occur on land. They are known as *bivalves*: *bi* as in "two," and *valve* as in "shell." The paired shells of the bivalve are generally, though not always, equal. They provide both protection and skeletal support to the animal held between them. In many species the shells are covered by a kind of dry skin known as the *periostracum*. A "hinge" joins the paired valves behind the umbo and is the back of the animal. To prevent the valves from falling open, strong muscles called *adduc-*

tors are firmly attached to both inner surfaces of the shells. Mussels and clams have paired adductor muscles, whereas oysters and scallops have but a single one. It is the large adductor muscle of the scallop which constitutes seafood dishes known as "scallop."

The term *pelecypod* is used alternately with the name "bivalve" for the same group of animals. It means hatchet-foot and refers to the large muscular, wedge-shaped foot of the digging bivalves such as the clams and cockles. Living in the mud, sand or gravel as they do, the clams and cockles must be able to move, if only to right themselves. To do this they extend their bladelike foot from between the valves to its full length, enlarge its end with blood so that it acts as an anchor, and then, by contracting the muscles of the foot, pull themselves toward the anchored end. The speed at which this operation is accomplished varies among the different kinds of clams. The razor clam (*Siliqua patula*) flies through the mud at eighteen inches in as many seconds. For most others, progress is slow.

Cockles are also able to use the foot as a springboard to bounce themselves across the sea bottom in search of a suitable site to dig themselves in.

Scallops have developed another means of locomotion. They neither burrow nor crawl, but swim by rapidly clapping their valves together, forcing water out of the mantle cavity in spurts of jet propulsion. The image created is one of a disembodied pair of dentures biting their way through the sea.

Mussels, so common in great numbers on wharf pilings and rocky shores, have modified the foot into a spinning device used to anchor the mussel shell by guy wires in much the same way as a spider spins a web. A byssus (filament-producing) gland secretes a mucus which flows along a groove in the foot to the point where it is to be attached. The mucous thread hardens immediately upon contact with sea water. A great number of threads are thus spun until the attachment is secure, often forming a great brush of stiff threads.

Moon snail (Polinices lewisii). No other snail of the Pacific Northwest will be easily confused with this huge snail. Creeping over the surface or plowing beneath the sand on its huge foot, the moon snail searches for clams and cockles, eating the meat by drilling a neat hole in the umbo (hinge) region of the unfortunate victim.

The moon snail shell grows to 10 cm (4 in.) in width, ranges from Alaska to Mexico, from the intertidal zone to 46 cm (150 ft.), and is preyed upon by its own kind and the sunflower starfish (Pycnopodia helianthoides).

The egg case or "sand collar" of the moon snail (Polinices lewisii) does not encircle the eggs as in a nest but contains a layer of eggs sandwiched between two layers of sand. The whole is held together by a mucous section. In midsummer the eggs hatch into free-swimming larvae which later settle and develop into the form of the adult.

Clam shells which have been bored by the proboscis of the moon snail typically bear a countersunk hole in the umbo region. Once entrance to the clam shell has been gained, the moon snail inserts its radula and eats the clam.

The rock oyster or jingle shell (*Pododesmus macroschisma*) has a special pear-shaped window in its lower valve through which the byssal attachment is made.

Rarest of all fabrics, the "cloth of gold" of the ancient world was spun from the byssus threads of a Mediterranean pen shell (*Pinna nobilis*). The material so produced is said to have had a silky sheen, and was olive-gold in color.

A structure often confused with the foot is the siphon, or the "neck," as it is known among clam diggers. Its function is that of a double-barreled snorkel, allowing the clam to sit happily buried in mud or sand while having access to the water above without taking in bits of sand, silt and gravel. One tube of the siphon brings water into the clam, and is known as the *incurrent siphon.* The other tube takes water out of the clam and is known as the *excurrent siphon.* In most species where a siphon occurs, the components are joined. Occasionally, as in the bent-nosed clam (*Macoma nasuta*), the siphons are separate hoses, the incurrent one being used to vacuum the mud surface in a large arc for bits of detritus which may have settled nearby.

Siphon lengths offer a valuable clue as to the depth where the particular species are found. For example, the little neck clam (*Protothaca staminea*) with

73

Cadlina luteomarginata. "Dorid" is the term given to oval, usually plump-bodied nudibranchs. There are two tentacles, sometimes retractile, on the head end, known as rhinophores. A circlet of gills surrounds the anal pore on the back toward the rear. The gills are known as branchiae and may be retractile.

A beautiful nudibranch that grows to 4.5 cm (2 in.). This species ranges from Vancouver Island to Baja California, over rocky areas. It feeds on sponges.

Leopard nudibranch (Diaulula sandiegensis) ranges from Alaska to California in rocky areas from the intertidal to depths of 40 m (120 ft.). Its color ranges from white to dark chocolate, the former most often found subtidally, the latter intertidally. Leopard nudibranchs grow to 8 cm (3 in.) and probably feed on various sponges.

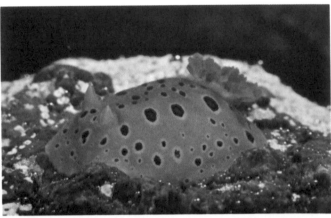

Dirona albolineata *grows to the order of 5 cm (2 in.). This nudibranch is distinguished by the many flattened and pointed cerata adorning the back of its near-translucent body. It eats small snails, ascidians and bryozoans. Most often subtidal near rocky shores, the species ranges from British Columbia to California.*

Striped or burrowing nudibranch (Armina californica). *No plumed gills or cerata will be found on the brown and white striped burrowing nudibranch. This species respires using two flaplike side gills, obviously an adaptation to its subterranean habitat. In the southern part of its range (from British Columbia to California) the nudibranch feeds on sea pansies; in the northern areas, on sea pens. The species is subtidal and grows to 7 cm (2.5 in.).*

Aggregation of hooded nudibranchs, possibly mating. The tentacled, fringed hood of this nudibranch often causes it to be mistaken for some strange jellyfish caught up in eelgrass or kelp beds. Rather, the "bell" is a feeding apparatus designed to capture small organisms floating in the water. No gills are present, only a number of broad spatula-shaped cerata down the back. The species grows to 10 cm (4 in.) in length.

John E. Ketcheson

Littleneck clam (Protothaca staminea). *Because the fused siphons of this clam are very short, individuals live just beneath the sand or gravel surface and are therefore easily harvested. The shells are moderately heavy, ribbed, and reach an average size of 6 cm (2½ in.) in diameter. The species ranges from the Bering Sea to Mexico.*

its short siphon occurs very near the surface. The geoduck (*Panope generosa*) has a long siphon allowing it to bury itself from 75 to 150 centimeters (30 inches to 5 feet) down. It stands to reason that because the scallops, oysters and mussels do not burrow they do not require a snorkel arrangement. In the latter group, water is drawn in one side of the shell and exits around the other side.

By and large, bivalves and other marine creatures, with the exception of marine mammals, breathe water as terrestrial animals breathe air. In most bivalves, the respiratory gills function to feed the animal as well as to absorb oxygen. A meal consists of tiny particles suspended in the water, such as diatoms, and minute plants and animals. Bits of food become trapped in the mucous coating on the gill filaments and are then moved along a groove by the beating of many tiny hairs known as cilia. Food passes into the mouth and along the digestive tract. This mode of eating is known as filter feeding. Not surprisingly, a great volume of water must be filtered to supply enough food, not just for ordinary sustenance of the animal, but for growth as well. It has been calculated that a good-sized Japanese oyster (*Crassostrea gigas*) filters 13⅓ liters (3½ gallons) of water per hour.

Life for most bivalves is simple, due mainly to the fact that they do not possess the equipment needed to have it otherwise. Of the senses, they have organs of balance known as *statocysts*, and will respond to touch by shutting their valves. There is no brain, only four pairs of *ganglia*, or nerve centers. The scallop is able to perceive its environment visually. When its valves are agape, rows of tiny blue-green eyes peek from between the shells. Rows of feathery, sensitive tentacles fringe the shell margins. Its many eyes have both a retina and lens, and are thought to register an image. Why the scallop is the only bivalve to be thus favored may be explained by the fact that the free-swimming scallops are the most mobile and vulnerable of all

bivalves and therefore need better sensory equipment than their cousins in order to avoid predation. It may be argued that the rock scallop (*Hinnites giganteus*) is an attached, sedentary species like the oyster and, therefore, should be exempt from special privileges. Yet, if one looks carefully at the upper valve of an attached scallop, near the hinge can be seen the impression of a perfectly formed scallop shell, about 2.5 centimeters (1 inch) in diameter, while the rest of the large shell is often irregular or grossly misshapen. What has happened is that, up to the size of a silver dollar, the scallop is a free-swimming, free-living creature. Then, for some obscure reason, it settles, attaching itself to some suitable substrate by the lower valve and continues to grow, though not with the same symmetrical beauty that marked its youth.

Scallops, as with all shell-bearing molluscs, enlarge the shell by adding shell material to the shell margins. Molluscs never shed old shells and regrow new ones, as do crabs, though they are able to patch holes or cracks in the shell if the damage is not extensive. Secretions from the mantle tissue below the shell add patching layers from within. Much the same mechanism is responsible for the production of pearls in mussels and oysters. Sand grains or parasite larvae are an irritation to the soft mantle tissue just as a crack or hole would be. The animal responds by secreting layers of nacre (mother-of-pearl) over the irritation, the same porcelain-like finish of the shell's interior. With time and more layers, the tiny bead becomes a pearl, and in the pearl oysters (*Pinctada*) is finished with an iridescent luster of great beauty. A cultured pearl is derived from an oyster which has been deliberately "seeded" with a small grain to stimulate pearl production artificially.

Most bivalves have gender, being either male or female; some cockles are hermaphroditic, and some, such as the native oyster (*Ostrea lurida*) and the Japanese oyster (*Crassostrea gigas*), alternate from season to

Cockle (Clinocardium nuttallii), *also known as the heart cockle, inhabits quiet bays of mud or sand beaches and is buried just beneath the surface. It ranges from the Bering Sea to San Diego, from the high intertidal zone to a depth of 10 m. The cockle grows to 10 cm (4.5 in.).*

Ron Long

season or annually. Many spawn year round, others only when "inspired" by the warming of summer waters. Whatever system is followed, there is no doubt that many bivalves have a tremendous potential for reproducing themselves. For example, a single female Japanese oyster releases 500 million eggs during a season. No mating occurs, the eggs and sperm are simply shed into the water, and by some mysterious natural predisposition many of them meet, the eggs are made fertile, and begin a free-swimming infancy which may last hours or weeks.

Soon, however, life begins in earnest for those larvae which have escaped any number of dangers and predation. By the time a Japanese oyster is ready to settle at two to four weeks, it is fully formed at only 3 millimeters (⅛ inch) in length. The settling of oysters is known as *spatting*, hence the name "spat" for the young oyster. An oyster will live in relative peace from two to five years before reaching a marketable size of 11.25 centimeters (4½ inches) when it will most likely be harvested. If left alone, it may live to twenty years. It is estimated that most other bivalves have a natural life span of between five to twelve years.

Bivalves are capable of producing a tremendous number of eggs, but not half, nor even perhaps a half of 1 per cent, grow to maturity. How impractical it would be in terms of available food and space if every year each female oyster successfully reproduced 500 million or even 1,000 more oysters. Predation is very heavy, not only at the juvenile stage, but at all life stages of bivalves. With the exception of the scallop which may be able to see its enemy coming and flee from capture, or the cockle which may bounce its way out of a starfish's reach, the other bivalves have less capacity to anticipate and avoid capture. For many, their only defense is to remain buried, close their shells and hope for the best.

Enemies are everywhere. Shore birds, fish, seals, mink, otter, sponges, starfish, octopus and man are

but a few. And, of course, the drilling snails are also hostile; not only the huge bulbous moon snail (*Polinices lewisii*) but the diminutive eastern drill (*Urosalpinx cinerea*) and the Japanese oyster drill (*Ocenebra japonica*). Both the latter species were accidentally introduced with the Eastern (*Crassostrea virginica*) and Japanese oysters (*Crassostrea gigas*) respectively.

Pacific Northwest bivalves are common to many habitats — the shifting sand of surf-pounded beaches, quiet estuaries and protected bays, exposed rocky shores, sand, gravel and mud. A few species even bore into rocks. The teredo, discussed in the following section, lives only in wood, while the scallops are largely free-living subtidal animals.

SOME NOTES FOR SHELLFISH-HARVESTERS

Theoretically, all clams, mussels and oysters are edible if one disregards taste, legal size limits applicable to some species in certain areas, and possible contamination of the meat by pollution or red tide.

Shellfish found adjacent to sewage outlets or industrial effluents should not be harvested. Such areas

Bent-nosed clam (Macoma nasuta), *like all macomas, has separate siphons. The bent-nosed clam grows to 5 cm (2 in.) and lives 10 to 15 cm (4 to 5 in.) below the surface in muddy sand from Alaska to southern California. It can be distinguished by the pronounced downward bend of the valves and the color of the siphons which are orange.*

Sand clam (Macoma secta). *Long separate siphons allow the sand clam to live well below the sand's surface, in depths from 20 to 40 cm (8 to 16 in.). This species appears to prefer clean sand. The incurrent siphon is very mobile, sweeping the surface of the sand above the clam, like a vacuum cleaner, picking up bits of food. Sand clams grow to 10 cm (4 in.) and live in sand from the intertidal zone to depths of 30 m (150 ft.) from southern Alaska to Mexico.*

Pierre Dow

Horse clam or gaper clam (Tresus capax) *is the commonest species to be found on tide flats of quiet bays. It may grow to 20 cm (8 in.) and has a large siphon used to transport water from above the muddy substrate to the clam 30 to 50 cm (15 to 20 in.) below. The horse clam occurs intertidally and below from Alaska to California. This clam is often confused with the larger, and less frequently found geoduck* (Panope generosa).

Razor clam (Siliqua patula) *is olive-green to brown and grows to a length of 15 cm (6 in.). It occurs on surf-swept beaches of the open coast from the Arctic Ocean to California in the low intertidal zone to several fathoms. The razor clam has a tremendous capacity to dig quickly into the sand below if disturbed in its resting place just below the surface.*

Edible or blue mussel (Mytilus edulis) grows to 5 cm (2 in.) and is found in masses on rocks, pilings or some other firm attachment. It occurs intertidally from the Arctic to California. Color may vary from black-blue to brown. This species does well in quiet waters of low salinity.

Pierre Dow

often have posted warnings. If an area is at all suspect, it is advisable to seek out one which is not.

Red tide is mentioned in the first chapter. It is a temporary summer phenomenon, though it may infrequently occur in winter, rendering many filter-feeding organisms, such as shellfish, toxic to human beings. The planktonic organism responsible (*genera Gonyaulax*) proliferates to such a degree that the water becomes colored by its density. The filter feeders strain the organisms from the water in the normal course of their feeding and tend to concentrate in their flesh a toxic material from the organism. If eaten, these shellfish can cause extreme intestinal discomfort. In particular, the butterclam and California mussel are to be avoided during a red tide and even up to a year afterward.

Shellfish harvesters are advised to contact local Department of Fish and Wildlife officials regarding legal size, bag limits and areas closed to fishing.

Some species of shellfish are rendered less palatable during certain periods of the year as a result of their sexual cycle. This does not mean they are poisonous, only that the flesh is not in prime condition. Oyster flesh becomes soft, thin and watery during spawning and for a period afterward in the summer time, quite unlike the firm flesh during the colder months. Clams are at their table best when in a pre-spawning condition during the winter time. In the summertime, after spawning, they are tough and less tasty.

California mussel (Mytilus californianus) *is a large black mussel of 15 to 20 cm (6 to 8 in.) or larger, and is found attached to rocks on the surf-swept open coast from Alaska to Mexico. The flesh is bright orange and edible. The California mussel frequently contains pearls; however, these are of no commercial value. A commensal pea crab is often found living in the mantle cavity of this species. Mussels are particularly affected by "red tide."*

Ron Long

Rock scallop (Hinnites giganteus). *The juvenile of this species is free-swimming for a time before settling and becoming attached by its lower valve. The upper valve is heavy, coarsely ribbed and often overgrown with encrusting organisms. It ranges from Alaska to California in the low intertidal to a depth of 25 fathoms. The rock scallop grows to a length of 25 cm (10 in.).*

One final word of caution to the shellfish harvester: take only what you need, and when digging in the sand or mud for clams always fill in the holes when the harvest has been gathered. Many other animals living in the sand, mud and gravel depend upon your doing so. If disturbed sand or mud is not replaced, many shellfish larvae and other animals may be washed free of their protection in the sand and die at the mercy of the surf.

Mussels. Mussels are characterized by a thin, rather kidney-shaped, dark shell of slate-blue, black or dark brown. They attach themselves to pilings, rocks or each other by many threads known as the *byssus.*

Scallops. Scallops, or *pectens*, are recognized by having the "Shell Oil" shell; a round fan with two "ears" at its base. Generally, only the large adductor muscle is eaten after being thinly sliced, gently pounded and then fried.

Oysters. Oysters are generally recognized by a white or grey-white irregular shell. They cement themselves directly to a substrate and do not have byssal threads. They are delicious eating either raw, stewed or fried.

Clams. Clams and cockles do not generally attach themselves to a substrate but bury themselves in the sand, mud or gravel. They do not have byssal threads nor do they swim, but they move using a muscular foot. They are eaten fried, stewed or in chowders.

THE WAMPUM OR MONEY TUSK SHELL (SCAPHOPODA)

It is possible that a particularly conscientious beachcomber may be fortunate enough to find a money tusk or wampum shell (*Dentalium pretiosum*) washed up on the beach of some Pacific Northwest shore. Certainly this animal will not be found alive intertidally, as it is a subtidal to deep water species preferring depths of 9.15 to 76.25 meters (30 to 250 feet) along its range from British Columbia to San Diego.

Estimates of tusk shell species range from 350 to 1,000 on a worldwide basis. Several species other than the above-mentioned are recorded in the region, for example, *Dentalium dalli* and *D. rectius.*

Unlike the elephant tusk, for which this group is named, the tusk shell is open at both ends. Burying itself in soft mud or sand with its narrow end just breaking the surface, the animal draws water in and out through the exposed opening, and thus respires. Tusk shells have no gills and absorb oxygen through tissue lining in the mantle cavity.

The submerged, larger opening has dozens of prehensile threads or tentacles emanating from it

Rock oyster or jingle shell (Pododesmus cepio). The shells of this bivalve are nearly circular. A large hole in the center of the lower valve accommodates a heavy byssus which anchors the animal firmly to a substrate. The rock oyster grows to 10 cm (4 in.) across and occurs from the low tide level to a depth of 30 fathoms. It ranges from the southern Bering Sea to Mexico. Like the rock scallop, the rock oyster is often camouflaged by liberal growths of plants and animals on its exposed valve. The flesh is bright orange and considered good eating.

Pacific or Japanese oyster (Crassostrea gigas) was originally introduced to the Pacific Northwest coast from Japan. It is now found intertidally from northern British Columbia to California over many kinds of beaches. It may grow to 30 cm (12 in.) and is the basis of the British Columbia oyster industry. A grey to white heavily fluted shell distinguishes this species from other local oysters.

Pierre Dow

which search the sand for tiny single-celled animals. Once caught in the threads, food organisms are drawn into the mouth and digested. Tusk shells have a muscular foot, as do burrowing bivalves such as clams.

These obscure molluscs are of interest not only biologically, but historically. During the early days of European contact with the native peoples of the Pacific Northwest region, the money tusk, or wampum, was used as one form of money and, according to trading records of the time, a 5-centimeter (2-inch) shell had a purchasing power equal to a shilling.

Wampum shells had been in use as currency by the native peoples long before the arrival of Europeans. Within their own trading system, value was determined by length. A 2.5-centimeter (1 inch) shell had little value; a 5-centimeter (2-inch) shell had greater purchasing power; and a 7.5-centimeter (3-inch) shell was of such worth, it was owned only by wealthy chiefs.

The wampum shells were gathered by canoe from known beds by using a tool designed to plunge into the mud and trap the shellfish. Naturally, the locations of such beds were closely guarded secrets.

Dentalia shells can be seen in museums on some of the ceremonial costumes of the coastal tribes. In keeping with the prestige and value of the shells, they were often incorporated into the design of dress worn for special feasts and dances.

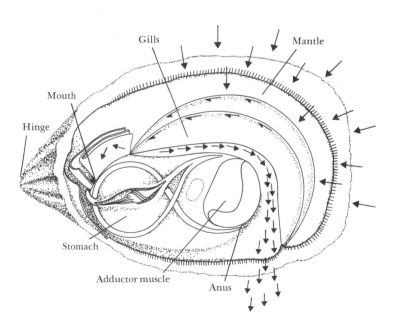

Cross-section of an oyster illustrating water flow.

81

Brachiopod or lamp shell (Terebratalia transversa) superficially resembles bivalved molluscs such as clams and
oysters. However, the two are in no way related; in fact,
brachiopods are closely related to bryozoans (moss animals). There are two shells, to be sure. These form the
back (dorsal) and ventral (belly) shields of the animal within as distinct from the two-shelled molluscs where the
shells cover the animal from side to side and are hinged
together dorsally. Brachiopods are typically attached to a
firm substrate by a flesh stalk emerging through a hole or
groove to the back. The stalk, or peduncle, is retractile
and able to rotate the shells. There is often no hinge, as in
the clams; the shells are held together by muscles.

Suspended food particles are brought to the brachiopod by water currents and are trapped in what looks like
a double coil or spring covered by rows of fine hairs, a
structure known as the lophophore. In some, fertilization
and early development of young takes place in a brood
pouch within the female. Free-swimming larvae are soon
released and after a brief, mobile existence settle and
metamorphose into the adult form.

Illustrated here is only one of a number of local
species. However, this is the most commonly encountered
and occurs intertidally. The valves may be heavily ribbed
or smooth, tending to give the appearance of there being
more than one species.

*Leather chiton (*Katharina tunicata*). A smooth, leathery black girdle almost covers the eight shell plates of this common intertidal chiton. The species is an herbivorous grazer of rocky beaches from California to Alaska. It grows to 12.5 cm (5 in.).*

CHITONS OR SEA CRADLES (AMPHINEURA)

The still, low profile of the *chitons* results in them often being overlooked among the rich and colorful abundance of intertidal fauna. This is despite the fact that at least 74 of 1,000 known species occur in the Pacific Northwest region from central California to Alaska. All chitons are marine and most occur intertidally or in shallow water on rocky shores.

It is not surprising that the chiton goes overlooked. It often bears many small plants and animals on its back and attaches itself so firmly to its grounding that it fairly melts into the environment.

The chiton takes the shape of a low, oval mound and bears on its back six to nine, but generally eight, flat shells which overlap each other in series from front to back like broad shingles. The shells are secreted by the mantle tissue beneath and present a solid shield to most of the creature's exposed surface. The shells are held firmly in place by a girdle surrounding the whole, much like an elasticized belt. The girdle may be smooth, spiny, hairy or, as in the case of the giant gumboot chiton (*Cryptochiton stelleri*), enlarged to such an extent that the shells are totally concealed by the thick gritty girdle. Chiton shells are not shed to allow for growth. As in all shelled molluscs, the mantle enlarges the shells at their edges as the animal grows.

The base or bottom of the chiton is formed entirely of a broad muscular foot. Using a combination of a sticky secretion and a vacuum-like suction, the chiton clamps down securely on its rocky substrate. Because the chiton cannot withdraw into the protection of a cuplike shell as can many other molluscs, it must rely on the tenacity of its grip to foil would-be predators.

If removed from their foothold, chitons will tend to curl inward forming a kind of cradle, hence the term "sea cradle" used to describe the chiton in some localities.

The chiton foot, as well as providing attachment, facilitates slow movement by backward waves which push the animal forward at a rate of 1.25 to 15 centimeters (½ to 6 inches) per minute. Observers will seldom see chitons moving during the day as they are nocturnal creatures venturing abroad in search of food when the light is dim, and returning to their "homing" area at daybreak.

Chitons are vegetarians. At the head end of the animal is a poorly defined head, beneath which is the mouth and a special feeding tool, the radula. The radula is a straplike tongue bearing many tiny teeth and is used to rasp the algal film from rocks. When not in use the radula is tucked away into a pouch leading off from the digestive tract.

The chiton lacks eyes or tentacles on the head yet is able to sense, touch, and perceive light variations via sensory cells held in pits on the shell plates. In this way the chiton "knows" when darkness has fallen and it is safe to search for food or when it must clamp down firmly to avoid being eaten. Other sensory cells in the form of chemical receptors in the mouth, provide the chiton with a sense of taste.

Respiration is accomplished by gills, located in two lateral grooves between the chiton's foot and its

Gumboot chiton (Cryptochiton stelleri) *is the largest chiton in the world, growing to 30 cm (12 in.). All shell plates are covered by a thick, gritty brick-red girdle. The gumboot chiton is fairly common yet difficult to see in the low intertidal zone of exposed rocky coasts. It ranges from Japan, the Aleutian Islands and down the coast of North America to California.*
▼

Lined chiton (Tonicella lineata) *grows to 5 cm (2 in.).*

▼

Brown chiton (Callistochiton crassicostatus).

Mossy chiton (Mopalia muscosa). Stiff, straplike bristles thickly cover the girdle of the mossy chiton. The species grows to 10 cm (4 in.) and occurs on rocky shores from Alaska to Baja California.

shells. Water entering these grooves at the head end passes over six to eighty pairs of gills (depending on the species), where oxygen exchange takes place, and exits to the rear of the animal. Absorbed oxygen from the water and nutrients from digested food are distributed throughout the body internally by a simple circulatory system.

Too little is known of the life histories of individual chitons to allow for broad, generalized statements about life span, reproductive cycle, and so on. It is known, however, that sexes are separate and fertilization of eggs takes place in the mantle cavity of the female. Chitons tend to be gregarious during periods of breeding and, therefore, the likelihood of a female drawing in sperm with the water normally taken in for respiration is greatly enhanced. As the water and sperm pass through and out of the mantle cavity, the eggs are fertilized. Generally the eggs are then laid either singly, in strings, or in a jelly mass.

The gumboot chiton, for example, breeds in the spring laying its eggs in two long spirals of jelly. After hatching, the free-swimming larvae begin to settle in a matter of hours and proceed to metamorphose into shell-bearing adults.

The gumboot chiton is the largest of all chitons, growing to over 30 centimeters (1 foot) in length and half as wide. It is common intertidally throughout its range from the Bering Sea to California, yet, due to its covered shells and large, bulbous size, it is often not recognized for what it really is.

A number of other, smaller chitons bearing the distinctive eight shell plates are very common intertidally as well. Among these are the lined chiton (*Tonicella lineata*), brightly colored with dark brown lines zigzagging over a lighter background; the mossy chiton (*Mopalia spp.*) characterized by a bristly girdle, and "black Katy," or leather chiton (*Katharina tunicata*), distinguished by a black, leathery girdle covering the edges of the shells.

TEREDOS

Humans view with benign indulgence and a stirring of gastronomic anticipation such molluscs as the butter clam, oyster, and abalone. How delicious are these succulent edibles of the sea!

It seems only fair that a group of animals such as these which have been so heavily harvested by many generations of hungry men since well before the time of recorded history, should have in their midst a creature capable of creating great destruction and misery for mankind.

The shipworm, or teredo, enemy of sea-going people through the centuries, is the mollusc's revenge. The shipworm is not a worm at all but a very unclam-like clam. Teredo is the name applied to some sixty-six different kinds of wood-boring clams, two of which are active in the Pacific Northwest. These are the giant *Bankia setacea* and the smaller *Teredo navalis*. These molluscs relish submerged wooden structures, be they wharves, boat hulls or logs. Such is their appetite and way of life that they bore and tunnel their way through all kinds of wood with frightening speed, rendering their wooden host a crumbling mass in a matter of months, if heavily infested. The period of 1917 to 1920 saw a famous case of teredo infestation on the North American Pacific coast, when wharves and jetties in San Francisco Bay suffered losses in excess of $25 million. Considering what the dollar was worth then, relative to its present purchasing power, one could say the damages incurred were substantial.

Teredos begin life like other clams as free-swimming larvae having a pair of shells or valves. For the tiny teredo, life will cease within weeks if it does not come to rest on submerged wood. If a wooden surface is found, the teredo, only 1/200 millimeter (1/5000 of an inch) in diameter, searches for an appropriate site to begin its boring. Using the edges of its fragile valves, the teredo pivots its shell to rasp a minute puncture in the wood and burrows beneath the surface.

Now the real work begins as the shells harden, developing filelike rasping edges (the better to dig a bigger burrow) to accommodate the rapidly growing teredo. With little external signs of their inner presence the burrowing takes place. By three months of age the teredo is chewing its way at a rate of 18 millimeters (¾ of an inch) per day. Generally, this burrow follows the wood grain, yet will shift in direction to avoid knots and bolts in the wood or a neighbor's burrow.

As the teredo grows it extends backward out of its shell, so that the rasping shells remain like jaws at the creature's head end with the body trailing behind in a wormlike fashion, hence the name "shipworm."

Like other clams, the teredo must provide for water circulation over the gills. To this end, a pair of long siphons, or tubes, extend from the tail end of the teredo to the opening of the burrow. Water entering through the incurrent siphon brings with it oxygen to be absorbed as it passes over the gills and planktonic particles for food. Water exhaled through the excurrent siphon carries away with it metabolic wastes and, during the breeding season, eggs, sperm or larvae.

At this point it is worth considering what is being done with the wood that the teredo is displacing as it bores further into its host. In fact, the sawdust is passed through the digestive tract of the teredo and by the action of two enzymes in the stomach is, in part, being converted into food for the shipworm. The teredo balances its diet of wood-chip soup with additional planktonic material strained from the water in the conventional clam manner.

As it bores, the teredo's mantle secretes a limy lining on the interior of the burrow. It secretes as well a pair of calcareous paddles known as *pallets*. These little structures are situated at the tail end of the animal, near the entrance of the burrow. When the siphons are retracted, the pallets are held against the burrow's opening, thereby securely sealing the teredo

in its home during unfavorable periods of water contamination or exposure. It is due to this protective device on the part of the teredo that attempts to eradicate teredo infestation through the use of external treatments have been such a challenge to those looking for a means of successful extermination. Shipworms are very sensitive to unusual chemicals, responding by retreating into protective seclusion.

Once a shipworm has penetrated the wood's surface it will not burrow to the outside, nor can it be induced to leave its burrow in an attempt to avoid noxious chemicals. Thus far the only chemical able to penetrate the teredo's defense is a solution of an arsenic compound. Otherwise, the only means of killing shipworms is to remove the affected wood from the water. Without access to water and the oxygen it carries, the animal dies of suffocation.

The control of shipworms is extremely important in the Pacific Northwest, particularly in areas where coastal waters are used extensively for the storage and transport of floating wood. Both *Bankia setacea* and *Teredo navalis* have caused considerable loss and damage to log booms in British Columbia, Washington and Oregon.

Bankia is a species found from Kodiak, Alaska, to San Diego, and is responsible for the larger bore holes frequently seen in beach drift logs. This species grows to 90 centimeters (3 feet) in length and can be as thick as a man's finger. *Teredo navalis* is half the size of the former and can be recognized by the smaller borings. This latter species was thought to have been introduced on the western North American coast from infected ships arriving here from the Atlantic coast. Now it appears to be everywhere.

Both local species of teredo are fast-growing and prolific. *Bankia* reproduces throughout the late fall and winter shedding eggs and sperm directly into the water through the excurrent siphon. Reproductive cells meet by chance and produce a fertilized larvae

Wood showing the burrows of the large shipworm **Bankia**
setacea.

which, in turn, begins boring within weeks. Interestingly, the *Bankia* shipworm matures sexually first as a male, later developing into a sexually productive female.

Teredo navalis is not so casual in its reproductive efforts as *Bankia*. The female of this species broods her fertilized larvae in her mantle cavity until the young are a few weeks old. This occurs in the late summer and fall ensuring that all offspring will be well-housed by Christmas. Like the *Bankia* shipworm, *Teredo navalis* breeds continuously for a number of weeks, the female producing nearly a million eggs.

As no one species of wood is teredo-resistant in all geographical areas, protection from this insidious pest continues to be a problem. Many submerged structures which have traditionally been wooden are now made of steel and concrete. Metal sheathing of wood pilings and boat hulls is practiced to some degree and other submerged wood is afforded protection for a few years by coating it with creosote. Because teredo infestation cannot be fully determined on casual examination, many submerged structures are tested by divers using sonic equipment to test practical strength. The forest industry employs testing stations where submerged wood blocks and known breeding habits make it possible to forecast infestations. This allows loggers to move logs to fresh water, treat logs with chemical sprays or otherwise pull logs before losses can occur.

OCTOPUS AND SQUID (CEPHALOPODS)
What has two eyes, ten arms, is 17 meters (55 feet) long and weighs many tons? It is *Architeuthis* of the North Atlantic, better known as the giant squid. (Perhaps it is in the Pacific, too, as remnants of the species have been found in stomachs of sperm whales caught off California.) Horrific and gigantic, the inspiration for medieval tales of the sea monster "Kraken," this creature does in fact exist, and is the largest of all living invertebrates.

Squid, octopus and nautilus comprise a major portion of a class within the enormous group of molluscs known as *cephalopods* ("head-footed"). Because they are molluscs, the squid, octopus and nautilus are descended from the same ancestor as the oyster, clam and slug. Just how this head-footed group deviated and developed is part of a tortuous tale of evolutionary trial, error and adaptation. No attempt will be made here to describe the how and why of this peculiar biological development. Suffice to say that the zoologists and taxonomists have examined the facts and duly established the relationships which provide a place for cephalopods among so many shelled cousins.

The fossil record shows over 10,000 different cephalopod forms, yet only 700 species exist today, all of which are marine. This may indicate that cephalopods are not destined to become a dominant living form. Though not a prominent animal group, cephalopods are unique in much of their life history, behavior and appearance. They deserve more than cursory mention. Discussion here will be limited to the octopus and squid. The shelled nautilids will not be considered as none occur in the Pacific Northwest.

Octopus and squid deviate in very many ways from the generalized mollusc form as typified in snails and clams. Most obvious is the apparent loss of the protective shell so tenaciously retained by the majority of molluscs, and the development of many suckered arms. The squid has discarded all but a simple internal stiffening rod known as the "pen"; the cuttlefish, close cousin of the squid, has retained just enough shell to provide bird cages with "cuttlebone"; and the octopus bears no vestige of shell at all.

However, the loss of shell can by no means fully explain the peculiar physique of the octopus and squid. To the uninitiated, these animals appear to be all head with far too many sinuous and suckered arms where a neck and body should be. What appears to be head is a functional baglike body containing all the

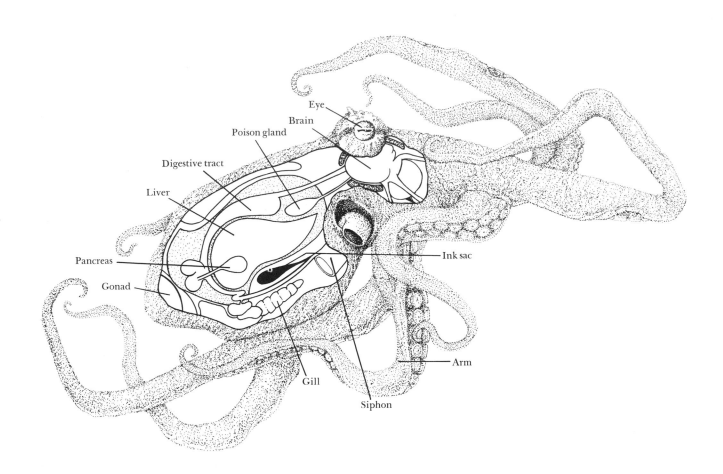

Eye

Brain

Poison gland

Digestive tract

Liver

Pancreas

Gonad

Ink sac

Arm

Gill

Siphon

organs and equipment needed by these creatures to survive in a competitive environment. Much of the reason for the strange appearance is due to the body's enclosure in a "mantle." The mantle covers structures such as gills, alimentary openings and so on by enclosing them in a "mantle cavity" and giving the body a smooth, globular shape.

An understanding of the "mantle cavity" is extremely important in comprehending and appreciating the cephalopods. It functions in locomotion (swimming), respiration (breathing), reproduction, and the elimination of body wastes.

Quite simply, the mantle is the skin on the outside of the body, excluding the arms. It can be likened

to a reasonably, but not quite perfectly, fitting bag which has been pulled over the viscera or organs to the point where the arms are attached. Imagine this bag becoming attached to most of the viscera leaving an open, ample pocket to one side. The pocket, or pouch, becomes the mantle cavity and, in the living animal, lies underneath it. The opening to the mantle cavity of a living octopus or squid can be seen as a flap just short of the arms, or in front of them.

But what is front or back? The end opposite to where the arms are attached is the rear of the body yet, when this most peculiar animal is swimming quickly, becomes the front, the arms trailing aft. The mantle cavity is directed to the bottom leaving the eyes on top. The mouth, situated in the center of the arms, is at the true front of the cephalopod where one would expect it to be.

Squid are adept swimmers, octopus less so. Propulsion in these animals is typically provided not by the arms but by the mantle cavity. Water is drawn into the cavity and the point of its entry is then closed off by a one-way, valvelike arrangement. Strong muscles surrounding the mantle cavity contract, forcing the water out through a funnel. This action causes the animal to shoot forward in spurts, in a kind of jet propulsion, with the apex of the trunk in advance of the legs. The outflow funnel is flexible and its orientation can be altered to change the direction of the animal allowing it to swim backward or forward at will.

Squid spend most of their time swimming and have developed lateral stabilizing fins because of this. Octopus are more prone to be bottom dwellers and are able to crawl over the ocean floor on their arms with remarkable facility as well as take to the open water with swimming motions.

Octopus and squid are carnivorous. They actively stalk live prey and, having somewhat different food preferences, exhibit different methods of capturing their prey.

Squid capture fish and shrimp "on the wing." To do this they use two long tentacles. The tentacles are much longer than their other eight arms and are capable of great elastic extension. In some species the tentacles are armed with clawlike hooks in addition to sucker disks elevated on short stalks. Initial capture of prey is executed by shooting out the tentacles which draw the prey into the firm grasp of eight waiting arms. The regular arms are also well supplied with sucking disks circled in horny rings.

Octopus do not have the squid's two extra tentacles for capturing prey. Instead, this creature stalks its quarry, generally during the evening hours or at night, and at the right moment descends like an umbrella over its victim. In the octopus the sucker disks are not stalked nor do they possess horny rings. Even so, they are capable of enormous suction and, once caught, prey is unlikely to escape.

Both squid and octopus have a powerful, horny beak at their mouth reminiscent of a parrot's. As the prey animal is held in the squid's ten or the octopus' eight appendages, the beak bites the prey. At least in the octopus, glands containing poison saliva discharge their fatal juices into the wound made by the beak ensuring a swift dispatch to the luckless victim. Food thus captured cannot be chewed with teeth and jaws as there are none, but a modified radula serves the same purpose. In most molluscs the radula is a toothed ribbon which extends out of the animal's mouth and is used to scrape algae off rocks. In the octopus and squid, the radula has broadened to grind flesh before it is passed to the digestive tract for rapid digestion. Waste materials from the digestive process exit from the body through the anus. The latter opens into the mantle cavity. Wastes are flushed away by water brought in to irrigate the gills which hang in the same cavity.

As squid and octopus hunt, so they, in turn, are hunted. Squid are eaten by all manner of fish and marine mammals, as are octopus, particularly when juveniles. The giant squid is preyed upon by the huge sperm whales. Captured sperm whales frequently bear large circular sores inflicted by the sucker discs during battles with the giant cephalopod.

Both squid and octopus have evolved some means of defense against enemies that are unique to their species. One line of defense is the ink gland. When intimidated they will eject an inky secretion from a gland located behind the anus. This creates a dense cloud in the water which acts as a smoke screen to allow for escape while also paralyzing the olfactory sense (smell) of a pursuing fish. As whales have no sense of smell it is unlikely the ink cloud would do more than visually mask a cephalopod from that particular predator.

Giant Pacific octopus (Octopus dofleini).

Gar Lunney

Many octopus have yet another protective mechanism in their capacity to work color changes. The mechanism is a series of pigmented cells known as *chromatophores*. By expanding or contracting different pigment cells, of brown, black, red, yellow and red-orange, colors can be brought into play that perfectly reproduce the background color of the animal, rendering it invisible when immobile.

Important in terms of hunting and in eluding enemies is the well-developed eye and brain of the octopus and squid. A long way from the simple light-sensitive organs of most molluscs is the cephalopod eye, remarkably similar to the vertebrate eye. The eye registers an image and, in conjunction with a fairly sophisticated brain, is able to distinguish between shapes and retain these as memories. In other words, the squid and octopus can learn and remember. Octo-

pus and squid are the only molluscs known to sleep regularly on a daily basis.

Octopus and squid do not hear but they possess sensory capabilities other than vision. Touch is highly developed, with tactile sensations being received by the suckers. Smell appears to be registered in small pits beneath the eyes. All senses considered, the squid and octopus are better equipped than any of their molluscan relatives to perceive the world in which they live.

Some years ago, octopus were thought to be infested with a long parasite worm, whose back end trailed repulsively out of the mantle cavity. It has since been discovered that the "parasitic worm" is the aftermath of copulation and is the end of a male octopus' arm. The losing of an arm, or rather part of one, is not as brutal as one would imagine because octopus have the power to regenerate lost parts as do many

Newly hatched Pacific octopus (Octopus dofleini). These individuals hatched after sixty days in 12.8° C. (55° F.) water. At hatching, the length of the mantle measured 3.29 mm (3/20 of an inch).

Pierre Dow

invertebrates. The arm, occasionally dismembered, is known as the *hectocotyle arm* and is designed specifically for its function in the procreation ritual.

Octopus and squid do not follow the impersonal molluscan habit of releasing eggs and sperm haphazardly to the vagaries of tide and wind, without so much as an acknowledgment passing between potential parents. The males personally present the goods to the female by hand, so to speak. Sperm is delivered neatly packaged in a long envelope known as a *spermatophore*. The arm adapted for this presentation bears no suckers on its end. Its sole function is to take the spermatophore from its owner's mantle cavity and place it in the mantle cavity of the female, where the sperm are released to fertilize from very few to tens of thousands of eggs in the case of the octopus, or hundreds of eggs in the case of the squid.

Female squid do not brood their eggs. Egg clusters are generally secured at various points on the sea floor and left, which completes the female role in the reproductive process. The eggs of these clusters are deeply embedded in a gelatinous substance which is thick enough to protect the developing embryos from fungus attack and disagreeable enough in taste and odor to repel would-be predators.

Octopus mothers are more solicitous than squid mothers. They attach their eggs in strings to the top and sides of their rocky dens, staying with the eggs and caring for them until hatching.

In a well-documented case of the giant Pacific octopus (*Octopus dofleini*) spawning in captivity, it was noted that spawning occurred forty-two days following mating. Thousands of rice-size eggs were laid, covering an area of two square feet. During the weeks that followed, the mother octopus manipulated the egg mass with the tips of her tentacles, presumably cleaning the eggs to prevent fouling. In contradiction to other reports, this mother continued to eat during the brooding period, though she blew away with her funnel any debris which happened to drift near the egg mass.

The brooding period, that is, the time between egg-laying and hatching, appears to vary according to the water temperature. The eggs of the giant Pacific octopus, are generally brooded for five to six months. The mother usually dies after they hatch.

In octopus and squid the egg hatches directly into a miniature adult and does not pass through a free-living larval stage. Depending upon the species, they have an expected life span of somewhere between two and five years.

The giant Pacific octopus is the largest of all living octopuses and may grow to a weight of 45 kilograms (100 pounds), with a spread of 5 meters (16 feet) from arm tip to arm tip. An unusually large specimen was reported to have an arm spread of 9 meters (28 feet).

The giant Pacific octopus is common from the low intertidal to depths in excess of 24 meters (80 feet) in southern British Columbia and northern Washington. This species is known to occur as far north as the Bering Sea and very likely is found as far south as northern California. It is seldom seen in the southern areas, however, possibly because the animals would be very deep due to their preference for cold water. For the same reason, octopus of southern British Columbia and northern Washington move into

94

Stubby squid (Rossia pacifica) *is small. It grows to only 7.5 to 12.5 cm (3 to 5 in.). It ranges from Alaska to California.*

Finn Larsen

deeper water in the summertime.

Adult Pacific octopuses live in rocky dens or crevices, the juvenile animals finding security in discarded cans and jars or under rocks. The den is identified by an accumulation of crab shells and other debris at the entrance, which indicates that the octopus kills its prey at the site of capture but does not consume it until after returning to the security and privacy of its own home. Though impressive in size, the giant Pacific octopus need not be feared in the wild. It is, by nature, a retiring non-aggressive creature.

In addition to *Octopus dofleini,* two other octopus species are known from Puget Sound: *Octopus leioderma,* which differs from the former in adult size 109 g (4 oz.) and apparently in coloration when small. The third species, also small, is presently being described.

Two other cephalopods occur commonly in local waters. These are the stubby squid (*Rossia pacifica*) and the opalescent squid (*Loligo opalescens*). The latter is common in open waters of the west coast of North America, and is seldom seen except when the females come inshore to spawn. This species is generally between 22 to 50 centimeters (9 to 20 inches) in length and is harvested commercially for food and bait.

The stubby squid is, as its name implies, stubby. Its body is thick in proportion to its length and the tentacles are short and thick as well, with a total length of 7.5 to 12 centimeters (3 to 5 inches). It can often be found half-buried in sandy or muddy bottoms from a depth of ten feet with only its eyes showing, ever watchful for potential prey. Groups may be seen swimming over rocky areas at depths of ten to eleven fathoms.

In total, twenty-one species of cephalopods have been recorded from British Columbia and Washington (thirty-four from central California to Alaska).

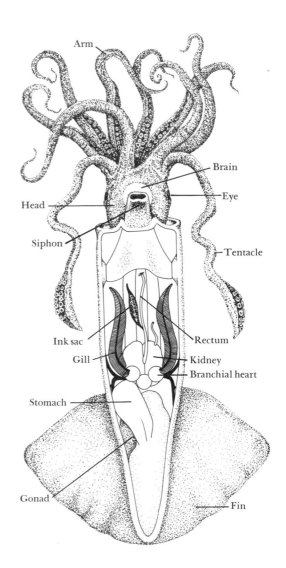

96

Spiny-skinned Creatures

Starfish, Sea Urchins and Sea Cucumbers

Echinoderms are an abundant and prominent group of marine animals. They are easily observed, as they tend, as a whole, to be large rather than small creatures. The phylum (division) is exclusively marine, and lives very successfully in a great range of habitats throughout the world. It is an ancient group having evolved a number of distinct variations on a basic theme. The latter will be better illustrated as each group is discussed. Features unique to the echinoderms are tube feet, and a radial (round) symmetry in the adult replacing a bilateral (two-sided) symmetry in the larva. Among the members of the phylum are the starfish, brittle stars, sea urchin, sand dollar, sea lily and sea cucumber.

STARFISH (ASTEROIDEA)

While far from being the most common seashore animal, sea stars have the distinction of being one of the most "noticed" creatures of the intertidal waters. They neither flee nor attack, they are simply there. Considered biologically to be a simple animal, they are very much alive and share with all other living animals, including ourselves, the problems of survival. They are born, they move, eat, respire, reproduce, respond to their environment and die.

Sea stars first made their appearance in the oceans 425 to 500 million years ago and are thought by some to be descended from a bilateral, ciliated animal, that is, a hairy creature having a right and left side. Just why the starfish eventually chose to have only a top and bottom, discarding any sense of front, back and sides, is not known. Most animals capable of movement become oriented in body shape in relation to where they are going and where they have been. A means of locomotion is developed that will push the body mass forward with a degree of direction and efficiency. The sea star, however, has the option of proceeding in any direction and still be moving forward.

There are more than 1,600 species of starfish.

This large and colorful group belongs to a larger group of animals known as Echinoderms, from the Greek meaning "spiny skin." Cousins are the soft and plump sea cucumbers, those spiny balls called sea urchins, and the delicately fragile sea lilies.

Like their cousins, sea stars are exclusively marine. Even though we find fresh-water shellfish, such as the fresh-water mussel, there are no fresh-water starfish. The greater number of species are deep sea forms. An edged sea star (*Albatrossaster richardi*) was dredged from 6,000 meters (19,700 feet) near the Cape Verde Islands. Fortunately, an abundant variety of these creatures occur in shallower waters and can easily be seen at low tide in many areas. The Pacific Northwest is particularly rich in species. All oceans of the world from the Arctic to the Tropics have starfish, but the greatest size and variety are found from California to Alaska. There they occur in a full color range from deep purple to blue, green, orange, brown, red, yellow and pink. The symmetry and beauty of these creatures is enhanced by the delicate patterns found on the upper sides of many sea stars.

A sea star is mainly arms, or rays, and most often there are five, but not necessarily. The beautiful rose star (*Crossaster papposus*) and sun star (genera *Solaster*) possess eight to twelve arms, while the sunflower star (*Pycnopodia helianthoides*) has up to twenty-four arms. The latter species is a giant of its kind having been measured at 90 centimeters (3 feet) across. The young sunflower star begins life with five or six rays, growing additional rays between existing ones as it becomes older. The warm water sunflower star (*Heliaster microbrachius*) develops up to forty-four arms. (All the better to hold you with, my dear!) Consequently size, color and number of arms of a specimen may vary considerably within a species. Biologists must, therefore, use other criteria in identifying the various species of sea stars.

They are clean animals. Unlike most bottom

Sunflower star (Pycnopodia helianthoides) is the largest sea star in the world and grows to 1 m (39 in.) across. Adults typically have 20 to 24 arms, juveniles have less, accumulating more arms with increasing age.
▼

Morning sun star (Solaster dawsoni) is distinguished from S. stimpsoni by its uniform coloration which may range from orange to yellow or blue. The species typically has 8 to 15 arms, usually 12, and grows to 30 cm (12 in.) across. It often preys on other starfish.

D. Kramer

Pierre Dow

*Sun star (*Solaster stimpsoni*). Color in this species ranges from pink, red, or orange with a distinctive blue-grey stripe extending along each arm. There are usually 10 arms and the species grows to 25 cm (10 in.) across. Food includes some sea cucumbers.*

*Short spined pisaster (*Pisaster brevispinus*), when seen intertidally often appears soft and flaccid, lacking the tough rigidity of its close cousin, the purple star. This indicates the species is less well adapted to intertidal life than* Pisaster ochraceus. *The short spined pisaster is an active predator on sand dollars and clams and its presence in a sand dollar bed will cause the sand dollars within a meter's radius of the sea star to bury themselves quickly. The species may reach gigantic proportions — to 60 cm (2 ft.) across.*

Pierre Dow

Pierre Dow

dwellers, the starfish does not serve as a home for algae or barnacles. If you look carefully at creatures found among the rocks at low tide, you will see a high population density. Many organisms are growing on top of each other; crabs, anemones, barnacles, corals, sponges, and so on, all exhibiting amazing tolerance regarding invasion of privacy. The tidy appearance of most starfish is due to hundreds of tiny pincer-like organs, called *pedicellaria*. These little claws protect the breathing surface of the skin, crushing any animal or larvae that would settle on its back. The large and beautiful sunflower star has pedicellaria large enough to see under a magnifying glass if you happen to have both available at the same time. Biologists use the size, kind, and pattern formation of pedicellaria in identification where color and size of the specimen are not definitive.

While the pedicellaria are crunching up some invaders, other debris is washed away in the mucus secreted by glands on the skin surface. In some species, the *Pteraster tesselatus* for example, the mucus secreted is so thick and gelatinous it has earned itself the name slime star. This mucus is toxic to fishes and in an aquarium many starfish cannot be displayed with fish as the slime secreted poisons the other tank mates or clogs the gills of the fish.

Most sea stars are carnivorous with voracious appetites, causing them to be viewed by the oyster-farmer rather differently from the naturalist. Encircling the defenseless oyster with its many arms, this predator pulls open the shell a fraction of an inch just enough to push its stomach into the shell. The meat is eaten and digested before retracting the stomach. Other bivalves are easy prey. The starfish becomes a "weed" in the oyster beds.

The Medusa of the starfish world, the basket star (*Gorgonocephalus eucnemis*) is a fascinating deviation from the starfish norm. The unusual shape is achieved by multiple branching of the five arms to create a waving basket of tendrils. Lacking pedicellaria and suckered tube feet, it is thought to ensnare tiny fish and other planktonic creatures in its basket of arms, and moves by undulating the rays.

Some sea stars, with crabs and other invertebrates, figure as sea bottom housekeepers, cleaning up dead and decaying sea life. Many are also cannibals. Some species living in shallow mud bottoms ingest mouthfuls of mud, digesting the organic matter contained in it.

The life-style of an average starfish does not require speed. The nearest candidate for long-distance runner would have to be the sand star (*Luidia foliata*) followed by the sunflower star, clocked at 180 centimeters (6 feet) per minute. Most are slower. The principle of starfish locomotion is similar to our own. It is a system of leverage or pushing the body forward. The thousands of tube feet found on the under surface of the rays are operated on a hydraulic system, the tube feet being hollow, muscular tubes filled with water. When muscles at the body end of the tube feet contract, the foot extends, pushing the starfish forward. The muscular tube relaxes, the tube feet retract, and so it goes. It is a slow method of progression but it works. The tube feet are also capable of great suction, a pull of 3 to 4.5 kilograms (7 to 10 pounds) having been measured on the sun star. This suction, created by the shortening of the tube foot, is employed for attachment to rocks in pounding surf and in feeding on bivalves. Suction is not the principal method of locomotion. How could the sea stars move over sand if it was? Contrary to common belief, starfish are able to right themselves if turned over, taking anything from a minute to an hour to complete the turn.

The water vascular (duct) system responsible for the operation of the tube feet has its partial intake on the upper surface of the animal. It appears as a small white plate, slightly off center and is called a *madreporite filter*, or sieve plate. The water contained with-

*Purple star (*Pisaster ochraceus*) is the most conspicuous of all sea stars in the Pacific Northwest. This species occurs in at least three color phases; purple, ochre and brown-black. A tough exterior protects the purple star from desiccation as it forages high in the intertidal zone for mussels, barnacles, snails and limpets. Individuals may reach a diameter of 30 cm (12 in.). During the winter the purple star tends to migrate to the subtidal level.*

Pierre Dow

in the body serves as a medium for free-floating cells carrying out much the same function as our blood.

One doesn't really think of a starfish as having a skeleton, yet it does. Without some kind of stiffening any movement using leverage would be impossible. The skeleton is composed of many small calcium plates, or *ossicles*, held together by a network of muscles to give the body rigidity and protection while remaining flexible. Species like the very common intertidal purple star (*Pisaster ochraceus*) have very rigid bodies well protected from exposure to strong sunlight and wave action. Those deeper water forms like the slime star tend to be more soft-bodied as the necessity for protection decreases.

Lacking a brain, starfish are still capable of co-ordinated movement and the ability to "sense" qualities of their environment. A cluster of simple eyes at the tip of each ray, called the "red spot," can distinguish between light and dark. How, then, do they find their food? Nerve endings originating from a central nerve ring appear to report chemical substances and vibrations in the surrounding sea. The tube feet at the ends of the arms seem to be particularly sensitive.

It would follow that parenthood is a casual affair; so much so that parents never meet, much less set up house. The sexes are separate and, barring dissection, cannot be distinguished as male and female. The reproductive organs are located at the base of, and extending into, the arms. Eggs and sperm are released into the water through minute pores and fertilization

102

Finn Larsen

is left to chance. If fertilization occurs, a free-swimming larval form results rapidly developing to adult form and establishing itself on the sea bottom. At this stage many young starfish fall prey to other organisms.

There is a tendency toward a greater measure of maternal responsibility in some deep water and polar sea stars. Two local species, the six-rayed star (*Leptasterias hexactis*) and the blood star (*Henricia leviuscula*), retain their young in brood pouches around the mouth until they assume adult shape. If a young starfish manages to survive the initial hazards of life on the ocean floor it can look forward to a life span of about four years. There are exceptions though, like the purple star (*Pisaster ochraceus*), believed to be the longest lived at twenty years.

Fortunately, what would be considered mortal injury to other animals does not necessarily mean demise for sea stars. They possess an exceptional ability to replace lost parts. All living things have some capacity for repair or replacement of lost parts, but the starfish, deficient in other areas, surpasses higher animals here. Species of *Linkia* can regenerate a whole new starfish from a single arm. Most other species require that a good portion of the central disc remain intact; even so, it is a remarkable feat. The mechanism involved has puzzled and fascinated medical science for obvious reasons.

Successful with a minimum of biological equipment, the sea stars established themselves long ago and have survived. They are unchallenged; for the most

103

Blood star (Henricia leviuscula), unlike many sea stars, lacks the tiny pincer-like organs, known as pedicellaria, which cover the dorsal (top) surfaces of most other starfish. Blood stars reproduce in January, the female brooding her eggs during this time in a dark protected place. The species ranges from the low intertidal to deep water and reaches a diameter to 18 cm (8 in.). The species may be red, orange, yellow or almost white.

Leather star (Dermasterias imbricata). The calcareous skeletal plates of the leather star are so small and deeply embedded in the "skin" as to give this species a distinctive smooth and slick exterior, hence the common name, "leather star." The approach of a leather star will cause an otherwise stationary sea anemone to release its foothold and move off. The leather star reaches a diameter to 25 cm (10 in.), prefers rocky shores and is frequently encountered in the low intertidal zone. A peculiar garlic smell is associated with the leather star.

Six-rayed or brooding star (Leptasterias hexactis) is inconspicuous and drab in color, though common and numerous. It is found under rocks intertidally and is full-grown and large for its species at 9 cm (3½ in.). The species is also known as the brooding star because during the winter, from December to March, females raise their bodies and stand on "tiptoes" holding onto the eggs, within the cup so formed, by their tube feet. Only when the young have developed enough to cling to rocks does the female relax, a period of approximately 40 days. Now flattened out, the female broods the young for another three weeks until they are 1 mm and fully formed.

A brooding female six-rayed star. If detached and turned over, a cluster of golden-yellow eggs can be seen living in the cavity formed by the peculiar hunched posture. Brooding behavior in sea stars is most marked in very cold water species and is observed in another local sea star, the blood star (Henricia leviscula).

Brittle star (Ophiopholis aculeata). Serpent or brittle stars, like the sea lilies are related to, yet distinct from sea stars. Brittle stars are distinguished by their small size and five, thin, snaky arms radiating from a distinct central disk. The group lacks pedicellaria, and whereas tube feet are present, these are not used in locomotion but for food-gathering. Locomotion is swift, compared to sea stars, and accomplished by rapid writhing of the arms; essentially two pulling, three pushing. Brittle stars are so named for their tendency to drop arms or portions thereof at the slightest provocation. Arms so automotized are quickly regenerated. Some brittle stars gather detritus and small organisms from the surface of mud, sand, or rocks. Others wave their arms "overhead" to ensnare suspended particles from the water. Tube feet on the arms under surface pass entrapped food particles and mucus "hand over hand" to the mouth. Unlike the sea stars, brittle stars are not able to extrude their stomachs out of their mouths.

Most brittle stars release eggs and sperm to the water with no brooding or parental care whatsoever. However, some brittle stars, including the females of the local species Amphipholis *brood their eggs.*

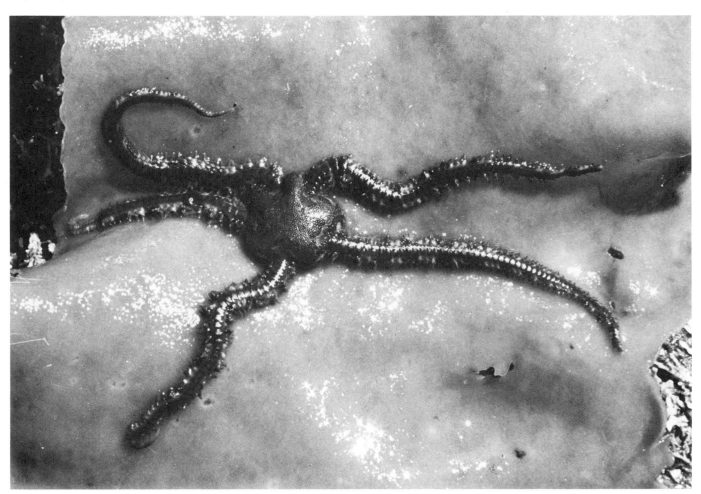

part their enemies being only themselves, occasionally sea birds and sea otters and, of course, man when they encroach on his operations.

Modern man is changing his world, affecting it in so many ways with incredible speed. The sea star exists, silent and slow, but in many ways a superstar.

SEA URCHINS (ECHINOIDEA)

Sea urchins are first cousins to the sea stars, though the close relationship may not at first be apparent in a healthy, live urchin. The animal bears more resemblance to a cushion stuck at random with a great many long stout spines than it does to its five-armed relative. However, one has only to examine the urchin's skele-

ton, or test, as it is called, to discover a pattern of five radiating divisions. Unlike the sea star with its scattered bits and pieces of skeleton, the urchin's is composed of many fused plates creating a single, somewhat depressed, hollow ball, open in the bottom center. Small holes for the passage of tube feet, and knobs for the articulation of the movable spines are arranged in definite radiating patterns over the test making it, with its great beauty and symmetry, one of nature's works of art.

At first glance it appears as if nature overdid it in the defense department. A few spines are very definitely a deterrent to some would-be predators, but does the urchin really need as many spines as were pro-

105

Basket star (Gorgonocephalus eucnemis) *is a most beautiful and elaborate creature, in the same group as the brittle stars, so pale by comparison. Five arms radiate from a distinct oral disk, branch, and branch again and again to create a net of arms. The basket star is attached to a substrate at its lower surface and does not, therefore, actively search for food. Rather, it raises its arms creating a sieve* to capture plankton and other waterborne organisms. Once food-laden, the arms coil inward to the mouth located on the upper surface of the oral disk. A basket star, having eaten, remains coiled much like a loose ball of heavy twine.

The species illustrated here grows to 30 cm (12 in.) and is found from 8 to 500 fathoms.

Slime star (Pteraster tesselatus) *gets its common name for the great quantity of slime exuded through pores in the body wall when disturbed. This is most likely a defense reaction, the taste, smell or texture of the slime making the star uninviting to predators. It would serve a dual purpose in washing away settling organisms. The species attains a width of 15 cm (6 in.) and is thought to eat sponges and anemones.*

J. Willoughby

John E. Ketcheson

Pierre Dow

Bat star (Patria miniata) *is easily distinguished from the other common "web-footed" sea star, the leather star, by its rough granular surface, very different from the leather-smoothness of the latter. The bat star is considered more an herbivore than a carnivore as are most other sea stars. It differs also in being sexually ripe year round, whereas most sea stars typically have a definite annual reproductive season.*

Individuals may attain a diameter to 25 cm (10 in.) and can be found in tide pools, under rocks in the low intertidal and in deeper water.

Feather star (Florometra serratissima). *Known as sea lilies or sea feathers, these creatures are related to, yet distinct from the sea stars. Some 2,000 fossil forms and 800 living kinds have been recorded, most occur in deep water. Sea lilies have no pedicellaria, no spines and no suckers on their tube feet. Some sea lilies are permanently attached to a substrate by a short stalk. Others are stalked as juveniles, later breaking free and in the place of a stalk developing a number of attaching tentacles. With these the sea lily is able to creep slowly over a substrate or swim freely by slow and graceful alternate dipping of pairs of arms or feathers.*

Sea lilies are suspension feeders gathering free-floating organisms and detritus in mucus covering the sea lily's feathery arms. Small movable hairs sweep food down toward the mouth which is situated where the arms converge on the animal's upper surface, as opposed to the sea star's mouth which is located in the middle of the underside.

vided? In the case of our local species the abundance of spines is possibly related to the feeding habits of the animals. Lacking the powerful, flexible arms of the sea stars to hold and subdue large live prey, urchins must exploit other less demanding food sources such as bits of seaweed which become caught by chance on and between the sharp spines. Seaweed so caught is passed "hand over hand" to the mouth by the tube feet which are seen as long threads extending from between the spines. Because the tube feet occur over the whole urchin body rather than exclusively on the under surface as in sea stars, urchins are able to utilize the whole body as an incidental food trap including the top, sides and bottom.

In the discussion of sea stars, pedicellaria were described as tiny pairs of jaws. Too small to be seen clearly, they covered the sea star's back and kept it clean and free of unwanted settlers. Sea urchins also have pedicellaria. In this group of animals the jaws have undergone some modifications better to suit the life and times of an urchin.

Rather than a pair of jaws, there are maybe three or even five, elevated on stalks enabling the **tiny jaws** to reach out and bite. Depending upon the species of the urchin, the pedicellaria may be adapted to special assignments. Some are designed simply to remove unwanted squatters, others to hold small animals for delivery to the mouth, and others contain poison and act with the spines as a protective device against predators.

Using pedicellaria for catching food may appear somewhat futile until one considers the thousands of fish and invertebrates releasing thousands of larvae, most of which are looking for a place to settle.

Aside from the passive acceptance of nourishment described above, urchins are not above moving about in search of food. They will graze on many attached plants and animals. In short, urchins are very much opportunity feeders.

Critical to the sea urchin's capacity to exploit a great range of animal and vegetable material as food, is its ability to chew the food enough so that it can be handled by the creature's digestive tract. In the sea urchin's middle bottom is a mouth. Hidden within is a most wonderful device known as "Aristotle's lantern," used not to light the way but as a multi-purpose chewing machine. The apparatus is so named because Aristotle described the five-tooth chewer as resembling an ancient five-sided lantern. The complete apparatus, a wonder of biological engineering, is composed of forty separate ossicles (bones) arranged in a circular fashion and moved by sixty separate muscles. The latter move the teeth out, in, sideways, or rotate them in turn like an auger. The teeth can be made to bite, scrape, chew or drill. Encrusting animals such as bryozoans and calcareous tube worms are defenseless against the urchin's teeth.

In addition, by lifting and depressing the lantern structure, water circulation within the body cavities of the urchin is maintained. Thus the lantern serves as a "bellows" to aid respiration as well.

Sea urchins move over the substrate using their tube feet and are supplemented in some species by the

Purple urchin (Strongylocentrotus purpuratus) occurs intertidally and deeper in wave-washed exposed areas where it frequently inhabits depressions scraped out of rocks. The spines are dense and short. Young specimens may be greenish in color, adults are purple and reach a size of 8 cm (3½ in.). Range is from Alaska to California.

Green urchin (Strongylocentrotus droebachiensis) grows to 8 cm (3 in.) and it ranges from Washington and north, also in the Atlantic. This is the local species of tide pools and protected rocky shores. Spines are short and blunt. It is thought to feed largely on bits of seaweed. Most sea urchins have a life span of four to eight years.

Pierre Dow

Ron Long

Sand dollars (Dendraster excentricus) grow to 8 cm (3.2 in.). See page 112.

Sand dollar test.

109

Red burrowing cucumber (Cucumaria miniata) grows to 20 cm (8 in.). The lowest intertidal zone from the Aleutians to southern California may reveal this cucumber secreted under overhangs or in crevices. The body is dark-reddish or brownish. The most outstanding feature is a crown of bright red-orange feeding tentacles.

A mass of feeding red burrowing cucumbers.
▼

◀ *Giant red urchin (Strongylocentrotus franciscanus) grows to 14.5 cm (6 in.), spines to at least 5 cm (2 in.), and ranges from California to Alaska. This giant red urchin occurs in a number of color phases from pink to purple. It is by far the largest of local sea urchins and is often seen in large aggregations, forming extensive subtidal mats in areas protected yet subject to good flushing action, like rocky channels. Some may be exposed at an extreme low tide.*

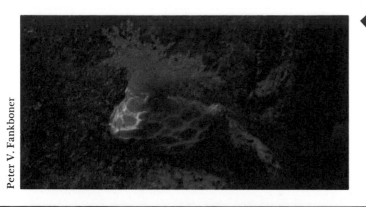

Peter V. Fankboner

Armored cucumber (Psolus chitonoides) *grows to 5 cm (2 in.), and is the most "uncucumber-looking" cucumber. Its upper surface is covered with hard bony plates, which overlap like shingles. Bright red feeding tentacles are located at the top and front of the animal, unlike most other holothurians. This species is almost sedentary, nearly always subtidal and an absolute delight to watch. It is found from California to British Columbia and possibly further north.*

Armored sea cucumber with food-laden feeding tentacle inside mouth.

John E. Ketcheson

Giant red cucumber (Parastichopus californicus) *grows to 40 cm (15 in.). This is an enormous cucumber adorned with many soft, fleshy horns on the back of its body. Though the body is typically red to dark maroon, the feeding mops are white. It is a subtidal species of many habitats. The giant red cucumber is often parasitized internally by snails.*

Feeding "mops" of giant red cucumber.

bottom spines used as stilts. Movements are seldom extensive, with many urchins returning to a home site for a part of each day. Other species on surf-pounded rocky coasts seldom move preferring the security of excavated stony cups in which they sit. The small purple urchin *(Strongylocentrotus purpuratus)* is commonly seen living this way. How the excavated depressions are made in the rocks is still a matter of conjecture. However, it is thought that the spines and teeth of many urchins over a long period of time are responsible for grinding out the holes.

If damaged, sea urchins are unable to respond with quite the tremendous regenerative powers as the starfish. Lost spines, tube feet and pedicellaria are replaced, and though damage to the test may heal over, it bears permanent disfigurement.

Sea urchins attract much interest in many parts of the world, not as a result of their unique shape or vivid colors, but because of their delicious roe. The roe is actually the ripe gonads of the mature male or female urchin and is reputed to be at its sumptuous best in late fall and early winter. The yellow gonads are eaten raw as is, or strained and then whipped to a creamy consistency to be eaten as a spread on toasted French bread. Locally, the giant red urchin is harvested for export to the Japanese market. Urchins

over 10 centimeters (4 inches) across the test are collected by divers and transferred to the packing plant where the gonads are removed. The roe is then dipped in a weak alum solution, washed, and packed. The price fetched for this delicacy on the Japanese market is substantial. This may be due in part to the belief by some that sea urchin eggs enhance sexual prowess. Yet just as beauty is in the eye of the beholder, an aphrodisiac's power is in the mind of the eater.

Those urchins whose lives are not cut short to satisfy the gastronomic pleasures of urchin egg-eaters may look forward to a fairly long, uncomplicated and unharassed existence. As a free-swimming larva or a just settled juvenile, the sea urchin undergoes substantial predation by starfish and many species of fish. But once established and well-spined, only the sea otter, some sea stars, and man are a real threat.

SAND DOLLARS

Sand dollars, or sand cookies, are essentially flattened sea urchins. The long, sharp spines and tube feet of the urchin are abbreviated to create a lush velvet coat on the animal's exterior. Like the sea urchin, the sand dollar has a single skeleton or test. It is reinforced internally by small pillars or braces to prevent crushing. The grey or white sand dollars found on the beach

112

bearing a distinct flower pattern of five petals are not live sand dollars but the skeletons of once living specimens. Locally, the living sand dollars (*Dendraster excentricus*) are dark purple to almost black in color and will seldom be seen lying exposed on the sand at low tide; more likely they will be secreted just below the surface.

When covered with water, the sand dollar digs one-third of its body into the sand so that the top two-thirds is vertical and exposed to the tidal flow. Thus exposed, it becomes a food-catcher trapping particles of food in the mucus between the short spines. But how does the food reach the sand dollar's mouth in the middle of its lower surface? Among the spines are cilia, short hairs which constantly beat and, in so doing, direct the mucus in trails toward the mouth. Like small tributaries joining a larger stream, the mucous tracts are consolidated again and again into five main tracts. The tracts are directed so that food particles landing on the topside of the sand dollar can be transported to the outside edge, over it, and along the underside to the mouth. As in the sea urchin, the sand dollar has an Aristotle's lantern of five teeth. The structure is much smaller in the sand dollar as would be expected considering the small sizes of food being eaten.

As the tide recedes, the sand dollar falls flat and, using its movable spines, digs itself into the sand until the seas return again.

Sand dollars are creatures of clean sand beaches and will often be seen in aggregations of many individuals. When one comes upon a group as the tide is receding, it recalls an overturned cookie box, the cookies lying helter-skelter, not quite in a heap. The reason for their grouping is not for the benefits of company in the sense we know it, but more likely to increase the odds of reproducing more sand dollars.

Like sea urchins and starfish, the sand dollars are separate sexually yet do not copulate or engage in any courtship activity. Most likely the release of eggs or sperm by one individual in the group stimulates others nearby to follow suit. By the simultaneous releasing of sex products the probability of egg and sperm meeting is greatly enhanced.

SEA CUCUMBERS (HOLOTHUROIDEA)

A sea cucumber may look like a slug's relation or a worm's fat sister with a bad case of warts, yet neither is the case. Oddly enough, what one has in a sea cucumber is akin to a transformed sea urchin, as if the urchin has been squeezed around the middle, so that the body is stretched upward. Spines and pedicellaria are absent, the skin is softened, and the skeleton eliminated except for a few scattered ossicles. The resulting on-end sausage has five strips of tube feet running from top to bottom, the same five sets of tube feet which the sea urchin inherited from the ancestor of the five-rayed sea star.

For a sea cucumber, standing on its mouth would be awkward, if not impossible for a body without a firm skeleton, so the stretched-out, softened-up, despined creature falls over on one side. Three of five strips of tube feet contact the surface and are retained as functional tube feet. In most cases the two upper strips of tube feet, no longer needed, either disappear or are transformed into decorative warts and fleshy horns. Thus lies before you the standard sea cucumber model, such as the giant red cucumber (*Parastichopus californicus*). Other species display variations and will be described as the discussion proceeds.

Resembling a large caterpillar, the sea cucumber bears only a faint resemblance to its symmetrically round kin, having acquired an elementary bilateral symmetry in having the mouth at one end, the anus at the other, and a definite directional orientation.

Some sea cucumbers are the underwater dust mops of the sea, gathering up bits of detritus, small crustacea, protozoans and larval forms using the sticky, moplike ends of specially adapted tube feet which surround the mouth. When a mop becomes loaded with food it is put into the sea cucumber's mouth and licked clean in the same way a child licks jam off sticky fingers. Many species are able to retract the feeding tentacles completely into the mouth cavity when not in use. Such is the case with the giant red cucumber and the small milk-colored, white sea gherkin (*Eupentacta quinquesemita*) found intertidally clinging to the undersides of rocks. The burrowing red cucumber (*Cucumaria miniata*) of the same habitat does not always completely retract its crown of bright orange-red mops and, consequently, is easily identified by their presence.

Not all sea cucumbers live in a rocky shore habitat. Some, mainly tropical species, live on a sand bottom, and others, such as the local burrowing sea cucumber (*Leptosynapta clarki*), live a true burrowing existence buried in the sand or mud. The latter species has little need of the elaborate feeding mops of surface-living cucumbers as it gains nourishment by digesting organic material taken in as the cucumber eats its way through the substrate in the manner of the earthworm. Like the earthworm, the true burrower performs a valuable function in shifting and mixing the substrate.

Most true burrowing sea cucmbers have lost their tube feet, fine for clinging to rocks but of little use in the sand and mud. The local species makes use of ossicles in its skin to help brace itself in its burrow as it retracts. For this reason the burrowing sea cucumber is rough to the touch, yet the skin is very thin. In fact, the skin is thin enough to be used for respiration. Most surface-living cucumbers do not breathe though the skin, mouth or tube feet, but through the anus. Water is drawn into a pouch, the cloaca, and is then dispersed internally through a many-branched network known as the *respiratory tree*. Gas exchange takes place across the respiratory membrane. Each tree-full of water is forcibly exhaled before the next load of water is taken in. Knowing this, an observer is able to discern which end of the cucumber is fore or aft, depending upon which is doing the breathing.

A sea cucumber's anus is an ample opening and an inviting refuge for assorted small crabs, flatworms and at least one species of fish. The pearl fish (members of *Carapidae*), a small eel-like fish of warmer seas, has a most interesting association: the juvenile enters the sea cucumber head first through the anus, breaks through the respiratory membrane and establishes itself in the host's body cavity where it feeds on the cucumber's gonads. The cucumber is not left sexless as the gonads can be regenerated. As an adult, the pearl fish is free-living, yet continues to recognize a sea cucumber's cloaca as a good place to hide when not searching for food. It has been found that the fish does not attach itself with any permanency to a particular animal but will enter any sea cucumber if need be.

A sea cucumber's freeloaders can be more correctly termed parasites, or *commensals*, depending upon the degree of charity unwillingly exacted from its host. The adult pearl fish could be termed a commensal, a commensal being an animal which is gaining (in this case, protection) through an association with another, though not to the host's detriment. A parasite carries the association a step further, like the juvenile pearl fish. In this case, one animal is gaining protection, food, or whatever at the expense of the host. When two parties are associated for mutual benefit the association is termed *mutualism*.

For the crab or any other creature taking advantage of the sea cucumber's cloaca for shelter and protection it must come as a surprise when the cucumber eviscerates and suddenly the freeloaders are thrust into the cruel world outside. To eviscerate means to throw the insides out. It is not simply a case of tossing cookies, but of throwing out the complete guts, usually via the anus. Once thrown out, the internal organs are not retracted. A revolting development; the organs become disassociated and creep about for a time on

Peter V. Fankboner

their own. New organs will regenerate in as little as nine days for tropical species or as long as three months in colder waters species such as the giant red cucumber. The cucumber appears to manage quite well without its organs while they are being replaced.

Why do they eviscerate? First, not all species are prone to evisceration, though a great number are. In those that do, it is occasionally in response to unfavorable conditions such as a rise or fall of water temperature, a fouling of the water, or for no apparent reason at all. As an example of the latter, it appears as if the giant red cucumbers eject their viscera every fall, as all specimens collected at this time fail to have internal organs. Perhaps they are undergoing an annual eviction of unwanted tenants or simply a renewal.

More frequently evisceration is in response to attack. A crab, lobster, or fish attempting to molest the cucumber becomes entangled in the sticky entrails. The cucumber detaches itself from the whole and departs.

Still, evisceration is a radical and inefficient response to predation. Some sea cucumbers, generally tropical species, have developed *cuverian tubercles* as a means of reducing the losses resulting from evisceration. The tubercles are tough, sticky, stretchy

115

threads which can be ejected out the anus to entrap the enemy. The threads are lost once ejected, as the internal organs would have been had they been ejected instead. By the sacrifc of the cuverian tubercles the viscera are saved.

A sea cucumber simply cannot go throwing its guts out every time the shadow of a predator looms nearby. Surely, attacks or potential ones must be a daily occurrence in the life of such a soft-bodied, slow-moving creature. One is left to assume the animal must be in possession of a secret weapon. Correct! Like the nudibranchs, many sea cucumbers have a nasty-tasting skin. In the latter it is the result of a poison known as *holothurin*.

South Sea Islanders and peoples of the Indian Ocean have long been acquainted with holothurin and its powers. Mashed or chopped sea cucumber is the main ingredient of a particular fishing technique. A reef lagoon or other suitable area is poisoned by the mash; the affected fish are then easily netted as they come to the surface. Sea cucumber poison is not dangerous to man unless injected into the bloodstream. As the cucumber bears no spines this is not likely to happen.

Man is a major predator of the adult sea cucumber. The animals are actively gathered as food, known in the market place as *bêche-de-mer* or by the Malayan term *trepang*. Cucumbers are collected, eviscerated, boiled to desalt and destroy the poison, then smoked, dried and chopped. Sea cucumbers thus prepared are used in the making of soups and stews, becoming trans-parent and gelatinous when cooked and reconstituted. It is unfortunate that trepang has not found favor with Western palates as it is nutritious, low in calories and high in protein (between 50 and 60 percent). China remains the largest market, importing 304.8 tonnes (300 tons) per year with a market value of five to six million dollars.

Sea cucumbers are thought to have a life span of five to eight years. Reproductive activity occurs annually and most likely involves aggregations of animals. This is similar to that of other invertebrates which shed their eggs and sperm directly into the water. (Most species are separate sexually, yet a few hermaphrodites occur.) Some brooding behavior takes place, as in the local armored sea cucumber (*Psolus chitonoides*). Heavy plates covering the cucumber's back are raised up, forming small cradle-caves for the developing cucumbers. Like their cousins the sea urchins and sea stars, sea cucumbers have bilaterally symmetrical larvae.

Sea cucumbers are among the limited fraternity of invertebrate animals able to survive successfully in very deep water. At 4,000 meters (13,123 ft.) in depth, 50 percent of the living organisms are sea cucumbers. A species known as *Myriotrochus brunni* was dredged from 10,200 meters (33,464 ft.) from the Philippine Trench. The how and why of such survival, living where others cannot on bacteria and nematode worms, remains largely a mystery. The sea cucumber's occurrence at such a depth is further testimony to its uniqueness.

Feeding tentacles of white sea gherkin.

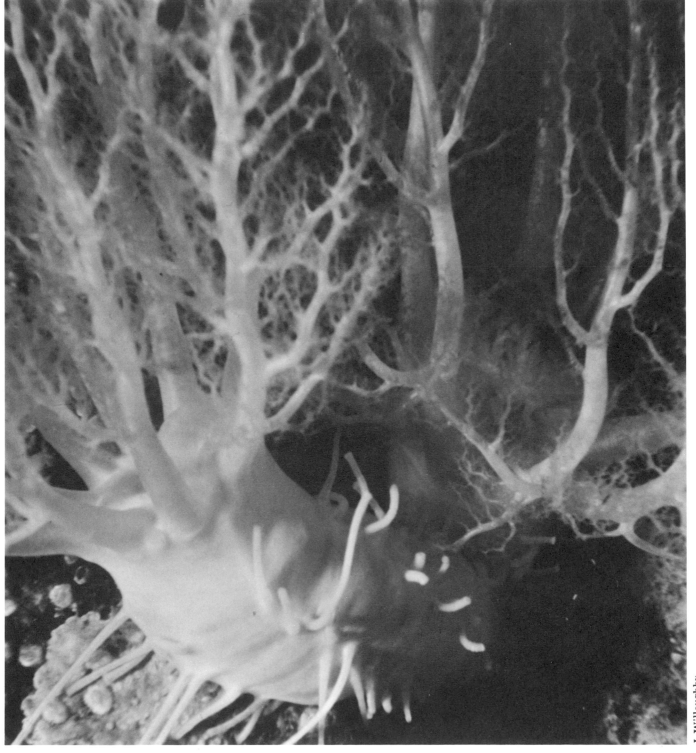

Sea Squirts

Sea squirts are so named for their capacity to squirt water when disturbed. Shaped like a potato and ranging in size from a pea to a large spud, they are typically found attached to some firm substrate and range from the intertidal to great depths. In solitary forms a pair of spouts, or siphons, looking like a pair of ears, distinguishes the sea squirt from other sessile organisms.

Sea squirts appear to mimic the life-style of sponges, lowliest of all many-celled animals. Both kinds of animals live out their adult lives in one location and both depend upon the bountiful sea to deliver food and oxygen. Yet, despite appearances, the sea squirt and the sponge are poles apart. In fact, the sea squirt is more closely related to man than it is to a sponge.

Ascidians, as sea squirts are also known, belong to the phylum *Chordata* of which frogs, fishes, whales, giraffes, mice, and humans are also members. Most *chordates* have a backbone, yet this alone is not enough to ensure identification. All chordates share three characteristics at least at some time in their life cycles: a *notochord*, a *hollow nerve cord*, and *pharyngeal clefts*. The characteristics are mentioned not to confuse the reader but rather to help clarify the terribly difficult concept of a sea squirt being more closely related phylogenetically (racially) to vertebrates (animals with backbones) than the sessile invertebrates it more closely resembles physically.

In order to appreciate this strange relationship between backboned animals and sea squirts, it is necessary to look at the larval sea squirt.

Newly hatched sea squirts develop into free-swimming larvae; but not the simple ciliated larvae one would expect. Rather, the larva is a tadpole-like form complete with a notochord which acts as a stiffening rod down the back providing skeletal support. A hollow nerve chord is located above the notochord and is expanded to a simple bulbous brain at its front end. Associated with the "brain" is a light-sensitive eye and a balancing organ. Pharyngeal slits open from the throat region to an atrium (passage). In more advanced chordates these three primitive structures would be later replaced by the more sophisticated structures: backbone (vertebrae), central nervous system and gill slits, respectively. As a tadpole, the sea squirt appears to be destined toward a bright future as some sort of vertebrate animal. However, after a brief career as a tadpole, the expected future is not realized. Instead, the larva glues itself head first to a substrate and begins to metamorphose into a stumpy adult. The notochord, nerve cord and tail are absorbed, and a saclike body with two siphons, or spouts, develops.

The specialized sense organs of the larva disappear in the adult and are replaced with a *ganglion* and a few nerves to the internal organs. While the ganglion could be considered as brainlike, if experimentally removed, the sea squirt is seemingly able to carry on its normal functions within twenty-four hours, unaware of its loss.

As a sessile, limbless creature, the squirt has no means by which is can search for and select food items. It must, therefore, depend on small bits of food to be delivered via incoming water currents. Plankton and detritus suspended in the water are drawn into the body cavity through one of the two top spouts. The incurrent spout is termed the *mouth pore*, the excurrent is the *atrial pore*. A sievelike structure known as the *branchial basket* is suspended in the body cavity, and it is through this structure that all incoming water must pass. Mucous sheets lining the branchial basket trap food which is then rolled into a rope of mucus and food that is then fed into the sea squirt's digestive tract for digestion. The branchial basket is well supplied with blood vessels and acts as a respiratory organ to absorb oxygen, as well as a food trap.

Nutrients and oxygen are delivered to the various cells of the sea squirt by a most peculiar circulatory system. A simple, tubular heart pumps blood first in one direction and then, after a brief pause, in the

Warty sea squirt (Pyura haustor) has a thick, wrinkled tunic which may be covered with debris and settling organisms. It occurs on docks, pilings, and rocky shores and grows to 5 cm (2 in.).

Hairy sea squirt (Boltenia villosa) has a distinct stalk joining the main body to its substrate. Hairy outgrowths of the tunic are frequently added to by detritus and small organisms. The species occurs on pilings and rocky shores from the low intertidal zone and deeper throughout its range from Alaska to California. Specimens range in size from 3 to 5 cm (1.5 to 2 in.).

Pierre Dow

▲
The glassy sea squirt (Ascidia paratropa) grows to 10 cm (4 in.) and is found subtidally from California to British Columbia. Its color is white with a translucent quality making this a very beautiful tunicate. As with most tunicates, it lives only one year.

The peanut sea squirt (Styela gibbsii) is wrinkled, hairy ▶ *and peanut-shaped, attached to the underside of rocks or pilings by a short stalk. It ranges from British Columbia to central California and grows to 7.5 cm (3 in.).*

John F. Quail

119

The broad base sea squirt (Cnemidocarpa finmarkiensis) on the social ascidian (Metandrocarpa taylori). Solitary sea squirts or ascidians do not necessarily occur alone, but when a number live together, they are not attached in any way. Social ascidians as in the many small red specimens shown here are joined, while new individuals are budded off from short runners developing at the base of adult specimens. The smaller species grows to 7 mm (¼ in.), the larger to 2.5 cm (1 in.).

D. Kramer

The sea peach (Halocynthia aurantium) is without a doubt the most attractive of local tunicates. It is the color of deep peach finished with a slick iridescence. Unfortunately, the sea peach cannot be seen intertidally as it is found only subtidally along rocky shores. The sea peach grows to 15 cm (6 in.) and ranges from the Bering Sea to California.

John E. Ketcheson

120

opposite direction.

A careful and patient observer should be able to watch this activity taking place in the local transparent sea squirt (*Corella willmeriana*) as it has an almost transparent body.

Sea squirts are also known by the term *tunicate* for the tunic, or coat, which covers the creature. The tunic may vary from soft jelly to a hairy covering or a smooth plastic exterior depending upon the species. The secreted *tunicin* which makes up the tunic is unusual in that it is a kind of cellulose, and is not known to occur to any degree in any other multi-celled animal except in the tubes of some sessile *hemichordates*. A more familiar source of cellulose is plants whose fiber is so well utilized by man in the manufacture of paper and cotton.

Some species of tunicates occur, not as individuals but as colonies of animals connected together by branching structures called *stolons*. Still others are embedded in a common matrix or tunic and are known as *compound tunicates* or *compound ascidians*. The latter often occur as encrusting jelly masses and are difficult to distinguish from sponges and bryozoans in

D. Kramer

their encrusting forms. The smooth, jelly feel of the compound ascidian's matrix is generally distinctive.

Colonial and compound ascidians reproduce mainly by budding off new individuals from the parent without the aid of eggs or sperm. Solitary tunicates are nearly always hermaphroditic and shed eggs and sperm into the water to be fertilized there. As the tunicate cannot move except to contract somewhat, the solitary creature has no choice but to live and carry out all its life functions including reproduction without any contact whatsoever with its kind.

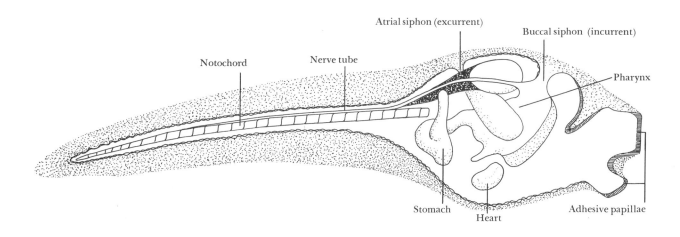

A free-swimming "tadpole larva" of a tunicate (sea squirt).

Fishes

The lives of fishes can be likened to those of birds. The great albatross lives at sea, is powerful and strong. The diminutive hummingbird flits from blossom to blossom sucking nectar. A grouse scratches in the gravel and weed for seeds and berries. The falcon dives to kill its warm-blooded prey. Some birds thrive in the Arctic tundra, others are of the forest, shore or plain. Each species, in adapting to its habitat, its food source and its enemies, has evolved habits and physical attributes which aid in its survival. Some are fast, others slow. Some fly, others walk. Some are timid, others aggressive.

In an underwater world of mountains, meadows and deserts, the same diversity exists in the lives of fishes because many of the same pressures to adapt and evolve in the air, are also present in the ocean, although the sea is a different and infinitely more stable environment. To quote Pierre Teilhard de Chardin, fishes are "an assemblage of monstrous complexity."

There are some 41,200 species of vertebrates — animals with backbones. This figure includes all the fishes, amphibians, reptiles, birds and mammals. A little less than half the total vertebrate species are fishes. Since their beginnings, 450 million years ago, 20,000 species survive today.

Just about wherever there is water (over 70 percent of the earth's surface) there are fish; from the intertidal to depths of at least 9,000 meters (30,000 ft.), from the warm tropics to the sub-zero Arctic. An almost inconceivable variety of habitats and food sources are exploited by the fishes.

How does one describe a group of animals so diverse, where the smallest member is an 11-millimeter (½ in.) goby (*Pandaka pygmaea*) and the largest is a 15-meter (50-foot) shark (*Rhincodon typus*)? Where body shape spans a range from flatfish to sea horse? Perhaps the best place to begin is by asking "What is a fish?"

A fish is a cold-blooded (*poikilothermic*), aquatic vertebrate. This means it is unable to regulate its own body temperature as does a bird or a mammal, and assumes the temperature of its surroundings. Usually it breathes by means of gills, has scales and possesses paired fins. A fish is mobile, has a head, definite brain and elaborate sense organs. For every generalization there is an exception and therefore one expects to find fish species that live for long periods out of water, do not have scales, lack fins, and so on. Space here does not allow for more than an acknowledgment that such exceptions do exist and in great numbers.

Ichthyology is the study of fishes. The word comes from the Greek *ichthys*, "a fish" and *logos* "a discourse." It provides the student with a system of fish classification reflecting in large part an evolutionary history of the fishes.

ABOUT FISHES

Like all other living organisms the fishes must respire, eat, avoid their enemies and reproduce themselves if their species is to survive. The development of an internal skeletal support with a movable, yet rigid, backbone, and, in most cases, paired fins, have endowed the fishes with a mobility far superior to the invertebrates. Concomitant with their structural sophistication has come a greatly improved nervous and sensory system.

Open ocean or *pelagic* fishes have streamlined, well-muscled bodies adapted to swift motion, with the tail, or caudal, fin providing the main thrust. Most highly developed in this respect are the tuna-type fishes with their almost rigid bodies and lunate (crescent-shaped) tails joined to the body by a narrow caudal peduncle (stem). Body muscles move the tail from side to side so rapidly it fairly vibrates, sending species such as the bluefin tuna (*Thunnus thynnus*) through the water at speeds of 70.4 kilometers per hour (44 miles per hour). The power and hydrodynamic design necessary for such speed can be better appreciated when one considers that water is 800 times denser than air. Salmon (genus *Oncorhynchus*)

Cross-section of a fish.

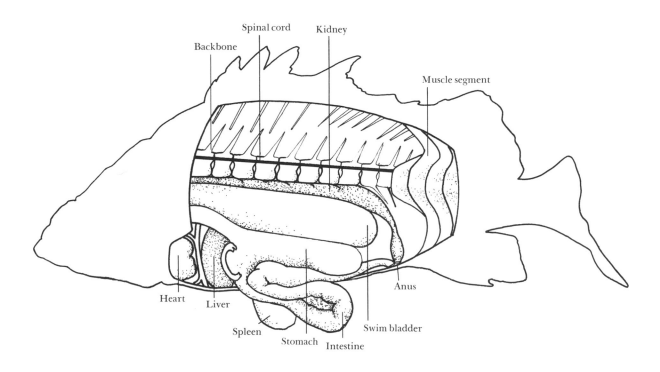

Backbone
Spinal cord
Kidney
Muscle segment

Heart
Liver
Spleen
Stomach
Intestine
Swim bladder
Anus

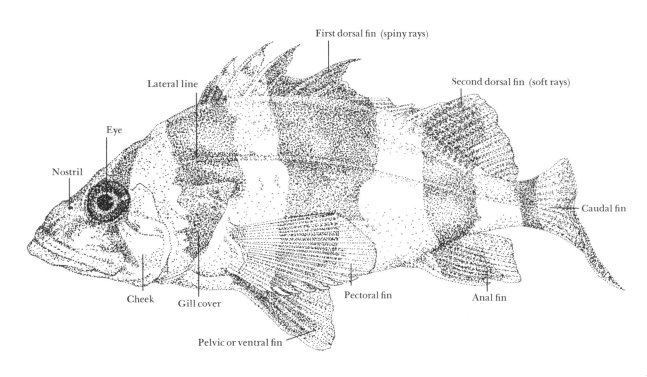

First dorsal fin (spiny rays)
Lateral line
Second dorsal fin (soft rays)
Eye
Nostril
Caudal fin
Cheek
Gill cover
Pectoral fin
Anal fin
Pelvic or ventral fin

can sustain 16 kilometers per hour (10 miles per hour) for short periods, about twenty seconds, and maintain speeds of 12.8 kilometers per hour (8 miles per hour) when cruising.

The majority of fishes, however, are not adapted for such speed of movement, but for maneuverability. This can be expected since most species are adapted to life in connection with the shore or bottom. In such cases the fins are generally large and in the case of the pelvic or ventral fins, have moved forward, almost under the head as in the sculpins (Family *Cottidae*) and rockfishes (genus *Sebastes*). Many shore and bottom dwellers use their pectoral fins like props or long fingers to pull themselves over the sea bottom.

Bottom and shore dwellers cannot be considered without mention of the swim bladder. This is a hydrostatic organ which acts like a float. Divers will imme-

diately understand its function if they think of it as a "buoyancy compensator vest." When a diver enters the water, the buoyancy of his tanks and wet suit are cancelled out by his weight belt, and he is able to descend as deeply as he chooses. If he wishes to remain at, say, 9.15 meters (30 feet) he must keep moving his fins to prevent sinking further. If he has a buoyancy compensator vest, he simply blows enough air into the vest to allow himself to remain buoyant at that point. More air will cause him to rise, less to sink.

Fish having swim bladders have the equivalent of a buoyancy compensator built into their internal structures as an off-pocketing of the gut. Where the swim bladder is connected with the gut, as in the salmon, the fish rises to the surface to gulp and swallow air. Where the swim bladder has become closed off, as in the rockfishes, the fish is able to produce or

Juvenile Pacific lamprey (Lampetra tidentatus). *See page 134.*

Finn Larsen

reabsorb its own swim bladder gases. For species which hang on rock faces, the swim bladder allows the fish to maintain its position in aquatic space without expending energy to do so. Often when anglers are fishing for rockfish (erroneously called rockcod), the fish they bring to the surface has bulging eyes and its swim bladder forced out through the mouth. The grotesque condition of the fish is the result of rapidly decreasing hydrostatic pressure as it is brought to the surface. Unable to reabsorb the quickly expanding gases in the swim bladder, it literally balloons within the fish's body.

Because sharks do not have swim bladders they must remain on the move to sustain their position in the water. When they stop moving, they sink. Some fishes which do not move up and down within the water coloumn, but remain always on the bottom, such as some sculpins, poachers, eelpouts and gunnels, have greatly reduced swim bladders or have lost the organ entirely.

To some extent body shape and body coloring are related. For example, most pelagic species such as the salmon, herring, and tuna are silver-bodied with counter-shading. That is, the fish's back is darker so that when seen from above by predators or potential prey, the animal will blend with the darkness of the water below. The belly is light, so that when viewed from beneath the fish will blend with the silver reflection of the water's surface and the sky.

Bottom dwellers, such as flatfish, are generally mottled or shaded to resemble the substrate they inhabit and are usually colored only on the exposed side, being white beneath. The sand sole (*Psettichthys melanostictus*) and many other flatfishes perfectly mimic the sandy bottoms where they are found.

Flatfishes are actually capable of darkening or lightening, and mottling, by expanding or contracting pigment within their chromatophores. Thus on a light, sandy bottom they will be a rather uniform, pale color, whereas on a gravelly bottom they will be

Pacific spiny dogfish (Squalus acanthias). *See page 142.*

T. Pletcher

mottled with areas of light and dark. Experiments indicate that the stimulus to alter the color pattern is visual, as blinded flatfishes are unable to alter their color.

Rocky bottom species often exhibit cryptic (protective) coloration as well. The red Irish lord (*Hemilepidotus hemilepidotus*), is nearly invisible until it moves — so perfectly does it mimic the algae- and sponge-encrusted rocks it calls home. Stripes, spots, and bars of all descriptions and colors occur on sedentary, rocky bottom fishes and not all coloration is for camouflage. In some territorial fishes, such as the tiger or blackbanded rockfish (*Sebastes nigrocintus*), the bold coloration, as in this species' rose and black stripes, acts as a warning signal to other members of the species.

Coloration cannot be considered without mention of body shape as well. Frequently the fish's body contour and posture are as much responsible for its cryptic nature as is its color. The flatfishes are an obvious example. These fishes begin life as regular, vertically oriented fishes, taking to the bottom and falling over to one side after a brief larval stage. The eye of what becomes the lower side migrates to the upper side so that whereas the fish is forever on one side, both eyes are on top. However, one gill remains on the bottom and the mouth develops a curious, distorted shape. Skates and rays, however, are truly flattened from top to bottom and have two eyes, naturally on top, and both gills on the underside.

The pipefish (*Syngnathus griseolineatus*) and tubesnouts (*Aulorhynchus flavidus*), with their long, thin tubular bodies, look for all the world like bits of sticks or grass. Neither species is endowed with much speed, which is unnecessary since their peculiar body shape provides effective concealment from enemies.

All manner of bumps, lumps, projections and spines of various descriptions obliterate the outlines of many fish species. A marvelous example here is the amazing headgear of the decorated warbonnet (*Chi-*

rolophis decoratus). Sitting among the rocks, with its head adorned with what look like little Christmas trees, the decorated warbonnet is well camouflaged from its enemies, yet able to dart out and seize prey before being recognized.

Spiny parts of many species, particularly the rockfishes, are for defense rather than camouflage. When threatened, the rockfishes throw their sharp dorsal (back) spines forward to repel potential predators. In fact, the rockfishes are related to the most deadly venomous of all fishes, the tropical stonefish (*Synanceja horrida*). The poison glands in the stonefish are associated with each of the thirteen dorsal spines. Should an unwary beach walker step on one of these, it is death within ninety minutes unless anti-venom serum is injected. Local rockfish, though incapable of such spectacular defense activity, can still give a nasty jab and an even nastier infection.

Fishes constantly secrete mucous slime from special cells and glands in the skin. This coating protects the animal from abrasion, infection and some parasites, as well as discouraging settling organisms such as barnacles, sponges and hydroids.

Under the slime coat there are usually thin, flexible scales arranged like overlapping shingles. Scales vary widely in shape and size; gunnels have such small scales that they appear scaleless, and poachers have their scales modified to hard, bony plates. The very largest of all fish scales are the palm-sized ones of the Indian barb (*Barbus mosal*), native to some rivers of India.

A fish's scales are not shed as the animal grows but are added to, growing larger with the fish. For this reason, where seasonal fluctuation of temperature affects a fish's metabolism as in the Pacific Northwest, growth rings like tree rings are evident on the scales and can be used to determine the age of the specimen (growth is rapid in summer, slower in winter). The ages of fish lacking scales may be calculated by using growth marks on the ear bones or vertebrae, but this

Big skate (Raja binoculata). *The Latin names for this species mean "two-eyed" for the two large spots, one on each pectoral fin. In British Columbia the big skate is common over muddy bottoms at moderate depths. Its total range is from southeastern Alaska to southern California. The pectoral fins of this large — to 2.4 m (8 ft.) — skate are sold commercially as fresh fish.*

A skate egg case or "mermaid's purse," as it appeared shortly after being laid by a female big skate (Raja binoculata). *This case was 22.5 cm (9 in.) long.*

Finn Larsen

Finn Larsen

method necessitates killing the fish, whereas scale counts are harmless to the fish as lost scales are soon replaced with new ones.

In commercially valuable species, determining the age of fish by using scale counts allows fisheries biologists to monitor catches and set quotas, so that catches do not exceed a species' natural annual and long-term increase.

Most fish "breathe" water; that is, they absorb oxygen dissolved from water. The water passes in through the mouth, over the gill arches in the pharynx and out, under the gill cover, or operculum. Though fish appear to be gulping water, two internal pumps, slightly out of phase, maintain a steady stream over

the gills. Because, volume for volume, water contains less dissolved oxygen than air, the fish gill is, of necessity, up to four times more efficient in taking up available oxygen than the human lung. Many fine filaments on the (usually) five gill arches per side present a massive surface area to the flow of water. In the mackerel, total gill surface area equals ten times that of the body surface. "Rakers" on the inside of each arch prevent suspended matter from fouling the gills.

Fishes are sensitive creatures. They see with monocular vision and some are able to discriminate a broad spectrum of color. The capacity for color vision

*Ratfish (*Hydrolagus colliei*). See page 145.*

John E. Ketcheson

is variable among species. Many deep water forms have been found to lack cone cells in the retina — the cells responsible for color perception — and, therefore, see only in shades of black and white. For many years it had been thought that sharks saw only in black and white. Experiments now show that sharks have cone cells in their retinas and are able to perceive some colors: yellow, for example.

Fish lack true eyelids and have no tear glands. Nasal openings in the form of paired or single pits "smell" substances dissolved in water. (It is thought the smell of a salmon's home stream is, in part, responsible for its ability to return sometimes thousands of miles to the waterway of its birth.) Fishes taste; that is, they perceive chemicals in contact, as opposed to those at a distance, as is the case with smell. Taste receptors are not limited to the mouth and tongue but may occur on the head and body surfaces.

Fishes produce and perceive sounds. The noises are created in various ways; using muscles in connection with the swim bladder or by rubbing hard surfaces such as pharyngeal teeth and spines. The function of sound production in fish is not yet firmly etablished but is thought to be related to courtship or territorial activity. Though this does not explain why the intriguing little grunt sculpin (*Rhamphocottus richardsoni*) makes its peculiar grunting noises when removed from the water.

Fishes have no outer ear, eardrum or Eustachian tube, but are able to perceive sound vibrations in water. A more important function of the auditory apparatus is that of balance, just as the human ear is the center of equilibrium.

Fishes have yet another sensory link with the environment — the lateral line which runs the length of both sides of the animal's body approximately at the middle and branches into three more lines in the head region. Its basic component is a *neuromast*, a group of sensory cells with hairlike projections forming

small pits opening to the body surface through minute pores. Each cell group is amply supplied with nerves connecting the lateral line with the brain. The sensory function of the lateral line appears to serve as a means of "touch at a distance," by registering pressure changes in the water. If one has ever watched a large tank of aquarium fishes being fed, all animals converging en masse on the food presented, it will be noticed that the fish never bump into each other or into objects in the tank. Perhaps this is due to the lateral line.

The same mechanism is at work in "schooling" fishes, when up to a million individuals, depending on the species, are massed together. Yet the school is more than a crowd of fish. Individual members are oriented in the same direction, travelling at the same speed, maintaining virtually equal space between them. The school moves as a single unit, all members turning or closing ranks in unison. There is no leader. Individual fish of a school are generally of equal size because larger individuals are faster than smaller fish of the same species. Consequently, schooling fishes will tend to sort themselves according to size and speed.

128

Herring (Clupea harengus pallasi) are small, to 33 cm (13 in.), unspecialized, schooling fish. They have no spines, no teeth on the jaws, no special features at all. Herring are abundant and their importance to man and the ocean's food chain is due in great part to this abundance. Herring are major food fodder for chinook and coho salmon, waterfowl, sea lions, seals, dogfish, lingcod and whales. Commercially, herring is fished for bait and reduction to oil and meal. There is also a smaller market for pickled or kippered herring and herring roe.

The herring occur offshore in summer, feeding on plankton, moving inshore during the winter to spawn on certain beaches used habitually year after year by the same herring populations. Spawning occurs en masse. Each female extrudes an average of 20,000 sticky eggs which adhere to seaweed, rocks and pilings. At the same time males release milt, or sperm, often turning the water milky for a great area when a large school is spawning.

It has been calculated that the 11 herring populations in British Columbia utilize 198 miles of shore in spawning, for a total of 2 trillion eggs annually.

T. Pletcher

What influences a fish to join others of the same species to form a school, and what are the advantages? The former is still unknown, but it has been established that schooling behavior begins very early in the life of a young fish, with tentative grouping and orientation attempts being observed in newly hatched fry.

Schooling is an effective adaptation, yet why it is so is still largely unanswered. Two thousand schooling marine species and another two thousand schooling fresh-water species, including both primitive and advanced forms, must find a definite advantage in the school formation. The school may serve to confuse predators, yet some predatory species school. The school may enhance reproduction where eggs and sperm are shed directly to the water, but some schools are composed of only one sex. Schooling may facilitate food-finding, yet only individuals on the outside of the school are able to search for it. Perhaps it is a means of conserving energy by employing group hydrodynamics; the exertion of each fish may be lessened because it can utilize the turbulence produced by the surrounding fish. Yet animals of the school's leading edge exert no more energy than would a solitary fish.

It follows that the greater sensory input of fishes over that of the invertebrates would necessitate a larger, more complex brain. Bony fishes are capable of learning and, through the use of memory, are able to develop relatively complex conditioned responses. However, it is difficult to find behavior in fishes unequivocally attributed to thought or reason.

Successful reproduction of a species is essential to its survival and, to this end, the fishes have evolved some of the most fantastic and improbable means of reproductive and associated activities imaginable. Space here will allow for only a few brief descriptions, and then only as they apply to local species. Species are generally separate as to sex; males produce sperm in testes, females produce eggs in ovaries. With the exception of the sharks and skates, and the live-bearing surfperches, brotulas and rockfish, most Pacific Northwest species are egg-layers. Some, like the lemon sole (*Parophrys vetulus*), release huge numbers of free-floating, or pelagic, eggs with the number of eggs released increasing with the size of the female. For example, a 30-centimeter (11.8-inches) female averages 150,000 eggs, and a 44-centimeter (17.35-inches) female averages near two million. These hatch within ninety hours in California and take somewhat longer in northern regions. After a pelagic larval stage of six to eight weeks, the young soles settle and metamorphose into flatfish. Another flatfish, the halibut (*Hippoglossus stenolepis*) may release up to 2,700,000 pelagic eggs, but does so only after reaching maturity at ten or twelve years of age. Female halibut may grow to 213.5 kilograms (470 pounds) and live to thirty-five years, whereas males achieve only a fraction of this

The chinook salmon (Oncorhynchus tshawytscha) is also known by the names of spring and king salmon. Chinooks over 13.6 kg (30 lb.) are known as "tyees," although the species averages 6.8 to 9 kg (15 to 20 lb.). Chinooks may spawn at any time of the year with the peak period in April. The young may go to sea soon after hatching although many remain in fresh water for a year. Chinook salmon spend more time at sea than the other Pacific salmon, from one to five years. Small third-year chinooks are known as "jacks." This species is highly prized in the fresh fish trade.

The coastal cutthroat trout (Salmo clarki clarki) is another "sometimes" anadromous fish. Those individuals which go to sea after hatching in a fresh-water stream, do so only after two or three years of living in fresh water. Sea run migrants stay at sea or in estuaries for a year or more before spawning in fresh water from February through May. The cuthoat are so named for the red slash on the underside of the jaw.

Coho salmon (Oncorhynchus kisutch) averages 2.7 to 5.4 kg (6 to 12 lb.) at maturity. A large specimen may weigh 14 kg (31 lb.). This species spawns in October and November and the fry emerge from their gravel nests in April. Young coho generally remain in a fresh-water nursery stream feeding on drifting insects for a year before migrating to sea. Once at sea, coho feed on crustaceans and later on other fish. Typically, coho spend two years at sea before returning inland to spawn. Some coho remain in the Strait of Georgia and are known as "bluebacks." These do not grow as large as the ones which range 1,600 km (1,000 miles) to sea. This species is known as the silver salmon in California.

Steelhead trout (Salmo gairdneri) is a most confusing fish with three races. All are spawned in fresh water but only the steelhead is found at sea. After a time in the fresh water stream of their birth, steelhead go to sea for usually two to three years where they feed and grow rapidly, attaining weights to 19.5 kg (43 lb.). Steelhead trout return to fresh water to spawn at least once, and often two or three times, unlike the Pacific salmon which die after spawning once.

Salmo gairdneri which migrate from the spawning streams to one of the large Okanagan lakes, not to sea, are known as Kamloops trout. Depending upon the productivity of the lake, and therefore the food organisms available to the fish, these may grow as large as the sea-run race.

Others of the species spend their entire lives in the streams or lakes of their birth, are typically small at ½ or 1 kg (1 to 2 lb.) and are known as rainbow trout.

Steelhead trout, Kamloops trout and rainbow trout, although all Salmo gairdneri, exhibit a bewildering range of color and size, dependent upon the local environments in which the fish develop.

Steelhead trout range from southern California to Alaska.

T. Pletcher

weight at 18 kilograms (40 pounds) and live to twenty-five years.

Lingcod (*Ophiodon elongatus*) are somewhat less casual, the female depositing her sometimes half-million eggs in rock crevices or under overhanging boulders. A large egg mass may be up to 61 centimeters (2 feet) long and weigh 13.5 kilograms (30 pounds). After depositing the eggs, the female departs leaving the male lingcod to guard and fan the egg mass until hatching takes place about two months later, when his guarding activities cease. As in the halibut, there is a sexual size disparity between male and female lingcod, the females growing to 137.25 centimeters (4½ feet) and 45.4 kilograms (100 pounds), with the males smaller at 91.5 centimeters (3 feet) and 11.3 kilograms (25 pounds).

Tubesnout (*Aulorhynchus flavidus*) males go one better. They not only guard eggs but build a nest as well. Tubesnouts are schoolers, disrupting their schooling behavior briefly during the spawning season when males establish territories and build nests by winding seaweed together with strong web-like strands extruded from the urogenital opening. Small bands of ripe females school above the nests eventually deposit-in egg masses not in, but on, the nest. The males guard these nests until hatching occurs a few weeks later. In this species sexes are of similar size, about 165 millimeters (6.5 inches) and are thought to have an annual life cycle.

The somewhat similar looking pipefish (*Syngnathus griseolineatus*), relative of the sea horse (genus *Hippocampus*), exhibits a high degree of parental care. In this species an elaborate courtship ritual is followed by a ripe female entwining her long, thin body around that of the male and depositing her fertilized eggs into the male's abdominal brood pouch where the young remain until 19 millimeters (¾ inch) in length. Once free of the pouch, the juveniles are on their own.

*The silver or surf smelt (*Hypomesus pretiosus pretiosus*) in British Columbia tend to be smaller than those of the same species in lower California; 22.2 cm (8½ in.) as opposed to 30.5 cm (12 in.). These are delicate, fine-scaled fish with very oily flesh and are fished commercially in British Columbia. Surf smelt are schooling fish and tend to segregate in schools by sexes. Spawning occurs inshore over protected sandy beaches throughout most of the year. At high tide for several successive days, the eggs and milt are released. Eggs become buried in the sand and hatch within ten or more days depending on the temperature. Surf smelt feed on a variety of small crustaceans and the larvae of other fishes.*

These few examples give some idea of the enormous range of reproductive activity in fishes. Naturally, when eggs are laid in the thousands or millions, it can be expected that only a small percentage will survive to maturity. Many eggs are destroyed before hatching through storms, dessication, fouling and predation by sea gulls, diving ducks, starfish, crabs and other fishes, to name but a few. If an embryo should survive to hatching, it faces uncounted terrors, mostly because of its small size. The hatchling becomes fair prey to any and all carnivorous animals bigger and faster than itself. Most larval fishes wait out the crucial period after hatching, as they gain in size and strength, among the shallow protected waters of eelgrass beds, sargassum weed and kelp beds. Because these areas are so critical as fish nurseries, it is essential that they be preserved and protected not only from physical disturbance but from pollution as well.

Fishes have life-styles just as we do, and often one is able to draw a fairly accurate, if not interesting, picture of a particular fish's activities and behavior just by knowing what clues to look for.

The kind of mouth a fish has can be very revealing. For example, fishes with whiskers, or barbels, on their snouts usually have an underslung mouth, like the poacher (*Agonus acipenserinus*) and sturgeon

131

(genus *Acipenser*). It can be concluded from this that the fish is a bottom feeder, perhaps a scavenger rooting around muddy bottoms for things to eat. The barbels indicate that the fish may live where the water is dark, or turbid, using the barbels to sense food where it cannot be seen. This is certainly the case with sturgeon living at the mouth of the Fraser River.

A huge wide mouth, accompanied by large pectoral fins, points to an opportunity feeder like many sculpins (*Cottidae*), often improperly referred to as bullheads, and lingcod (*Ophiodon elongatus*). These fish are not fast predators but move in short bursts to snatch in their huge maws anything edible that comes along such as fish, crabs and shrimp. In very deep sea fish, the whole animal becomes mouth — an adaptation for capturing anything where food is scarce and meals are few and far between.

A small forward-positioned mouth on a streamlined body points to a fast, open water predator such as the salmon (genus *Oncorhynchus*), or tuna. Here the mouth is armed with many fine, sharp teeth, so efficient for capturing prey "on the wing." For these

Large pink or yellowish eggs of the plainfin midshipman are frequently seen on the undersides of rocks during the early summer. These are guarded by the male until hatching. During this two-to-three-week period the adult fasts.

Flathead clingfish (Gobiesox meandricus) are found when turning over large rocks in the intertidal. The flathead clingfish remains attached to the underside of its rock by a sucker disk created by a modification of the pectoral and pelvic fins. The species looks like highly polished agate or marble, grows to 12.2 cm (6 in.) and feeds on small crustaceans and molluscs. The flathead clingfish ranges from southern California to southeast Alaska.

Pacific tomcod (Microgadus proximus). Many local fishes are referred to as "cods," yet only four species of true codfishes (family Gadidae) occur in the Pacific Northwest. The Pacific tomcod is one of these fishes. True codfishes are distinguished by having three separate dorsal (back) fins. The Pacific tomcod grows to 30 cm (12 in.) and is well regarded as a table fish. The species ranges from central California to the Bering Sea.

Finn Larsen

The blackbelly eelpout (Lycodopsis pacifica) is eel-like in appearance having a long slender body and a single, unbroken fin following down the back, over the tail and extending up the underside as far as the anus. Blackbelly eelpouts feed on a variety of organisms: small crustaceans, worms, and brittle stars. They grow to 46 cm (18 in.) and range over muddy bottoms from Baja California, to the Gulf of Alaska between 10 and 120 fathoms.

The tubesnout (Aulorhynchus flavidus) propels itself with rapid wavy movements of the dorsal (back) and caudal (tail) fins. It is a schooling fish, generally of quiet waters. The species feeds on small free-living organisms which it captures by snapping its mouth as it moves in forward lunges. Tubesnouts grow to 17.7 cm (7 in.) and range from Alaska to California. Nesting behavior of the tubesnout is described under the general description of fishes.

133

*Bay pipefish (*Syngnathus griseolineatus*). Though the tubesnout and pipefish are similar in appearance they are not related. The pipefish is distinguished by having a body wrapped in bony plates and by lacking pectoral fins.*

The female pipefish transfers her eggs to the male's abdominal brood pouch. There the eggs remain and develop until hatching. An elaborate courtship display precedes mating.

Pipefish frequent eelgrass beds, wharves and shore pilings where they move in short jerky thrusts sucking small organisms into their mouths through a long tubular beak. The species ranges from central California to southeastern Alaska and reaches a length of 33 cm (13 in.).

Pierre Dow

fish their best offense is speed; a large mouth, as in the lingcod, would only get in the way and slow them down by interfering with the streamlined design of their bodies.

Anchovy (*Engraulis mordax*) and herring (genus *Clupea*) are streamlined fish but have large extensible mouths that can be dropped open, becoming great plankton scoops. The peculiar sharp nose, stubby body and finger-like pectoral fins of the grunt sculpin (*Rhamphocottus richardsoni*) indicate that it is a slow-moving bottom species which feeds by poking in among barnacles and rocks for small worms and other invertebrates.

The position of a fish's eyes provide yet another clue to possible life-styles. Eyes positioned low and flush to the sides of the head point to a streamlined and, therefore, fast-moving species — again, as in the salmon. Eyes positioned high on the head, or even raised, as in the flatfishes or staghorn sculpin (*Leptocottus armatus*), suggest that these are fish which burrow into the sand or mud to conceal their presence, with only their eyes roving over the sea floor for potential prey.

Examples are endless and the reader is encouraged to watch fish as Sherlock Holmes would, looking for clues to where the suspect has been and what it has been doing.

FISHES WITHOUT JAWS (AGNATHA)
Two very unlovely aquatic vertebrates barely make the grade as fish. These are the hagfish and the lamprey (*cyclostomes* or *agnatha*) of which two species each occur in the Pacific Northwest. Superficially eel-like, with large, round, fleshy sucking mouths at one end and anuses at the other, these creatures exist as scavengers, parasites and predators on larger fish. They have no jaws, no paired fins, no scales and, in the hagfish, no obvious eyes. There are gill pouches: six to fourteen in the hagfish, seven in the lamprey.

The hagfish attacks its victim from the inside

Threespine stickleback (Gasterosteus aculeatus) is a small (to 10 cm [4 in.]), silvery fish generously distributed throughout temperate northern areas in both fresh and salt water. In the latter, they occur in brackish harbors, other coastal areas and far out at sea. Marine sticklebacks are considered to be anadromous fishes returning to fresh water to spawn. Male sticklebacks establish territories during the breeding season, constructing elaborate nests of aquatic plants. A courtship ritual follows the arrival of an egg-laden female. She deposits her 50 to 200 eggs in the nest which are then fertilized by the male. He remains to guard and care for the eggs until hatching. Newly hatched young remain with the male for a short time and then disperse. The cycle may then repeat itself with the male building a new nest. Female sticklebacks do not take part in the parental care of young.

Threespine sticklebacks are important forage for many larger predacious fishes such as the trouts, pike and some salmon.

Finn Larsen

T. Pletcher

Shiner seaperch (Cymatogaster aggregata). Children delight in fishing for this shiner from wharves using mussel-baited hooks. The species has large scales and is always shiny, though the color may range from bright silver to almost black for males during the breeding season from April to July. Females are larger than males right from birth. Unlike most other fishes, the ambiotocids (shiners, seaperches and surfperches) are born alive as miniatures of the adults.

Pierre Dow

Pile seaperch (Rhacochilus vacca), as the common name indicates, frequents wharves and pilings. A favored food is mussels which are eaten whole, shells included, later to be voided in the feces in mucous casings. Pile seaperch can be distinguished from other seaperch of the same habitat by the higher, sail-like back half of the dorsal fin. Adults are dark grey or brown above with silvery bellies and sides. Young pile seaperch have dark vertical bars. Adults grow to 44.2 cm (17½ in.) and range from northern Baja California, to southeastern Alaska.

Cockscomb prickleback (Anoplarchus purpurescens) *is the most common eel-like fish to be found under rocks at low tide along sheltered coasts. Its common name is inspired by the "cockscomb" on the head. During the winter a female will lay about 2,700 eggs among the rocks. She guards these until hatching. Individual cockscombs travel little, remaining within a 15 m (50 ft.) area most of their lives. The species reaches a length of 20 cm (7¾ in.) and occurs in variable shades of grey, brown, olive and almost black. It ranges from California to Alaska.*

Snake prickleback (Lumpenus sagitta). *This species may be encountered when fishing as it will take a baited hook. Unlike most pricklebacks, this one will remain out in the open near weeded areas and is not as secretive as its cousins. It may move in surprising bursts of speed when capturing prey. It grows to 51 cm (20 in.).*

Decorated warbonnet (Chirolophis decoratus) is subtidal occurring at depths from 18 to 91 m (50 to 270 ft.) and is larger and more robust than the other pricklebacks and gunnels described here. The bizarre head ornament serves to camouflage the fish from its enemies and its potential prey as it sits among growths of algae and hydroids. Warbonnets grow to 42 cm (16.5 in.) and are marked in tan and brown. The species occurs in inshore waters from Washington to the Aleutians.
▼

Crescent gunnel (Pholis laeta) is an eel-like fish, but not an eel. It is common under rocks, in tide pools and to depths of 55 to 73 m (160 to 220 ft.). It is named for the many crescent-shaped markings on the dorsal fin against a body ground color of yellowish-green. The scientific name is a Greek and Latin combination meaning "one who lies joyfully in wait." The species grows to 25 cm (10 in.) and ranges from northern California to the Bering Sea and through the Aleutians.

Finn Larsen

Finn Larsen

Crested goby (Coryphopterus nicholsi) *can be found in tide pools and shallow water from Baja California, to northern British Columbia. Adults are territorial and have a well-developed courtship ritual. Crested gobies feed on small crustaceans and worms and grow to a length of 12 cm (5 in.).*

having entered through the mouth or anus, and literally eats it from the inside out. It first digests the internal organs, then the muscle tissues of the living or dead host fish. Eventually all that remains is the victim's empty skin. Cod, lingcod, flounder, salmon and dogfish are commonly infested with this pest. One dogfish skin was found to contain four hagfish and, as the mature hagfish may be over 63.5 centimeters (2 feet) in length, hosting four of the creatures is no small feat. Not surprisingly, the hagfish is a serious nuisance to fishing operations.

The local species, the black hagfish (*Eptatretus deani*) and the Pacific hagfish (*Eptatretus scouti*), range from southern California to southeast Alaska. Eggs of the hagfish are few and large. Unlike the lampreys, hagfish do not go through a metamorphosis and they are strictly marine.

Although nearly the same size as the local species of hagfish, the Pacific lamprey (*Lampetra tridentatus*) is easily distinguished from the former by the presence of eyes and two fin folds on the back.

This species attacks its victim from the outside, not from the inside. Firmly attaching itself to a host fish's skin, the lamprey gradually rasps a hole through it with sharp, horny teeth. Once so attached, the lamprey is in perpetual association with food, sucking the host's body fluids and tissues.

After an undetermined number of years at sea as a parasite on larger fishes, the Pacific lamprey returns to a fresh-water stream some time between July and October. The following spring, pairs of lampreys dig nests, spawn and die. Within two to four weeks a new generation of potential parasites have hatched as larvae. These are carried downstream to pools where they bury themselves in the mud. For five years the blind, wormlike larvae live here eating diatoms (algae) and other small organisms, until at 11 centimeters (4.5 inches), they transform into the adult form and go to sea.

China rockfish (Sebastes nebulosus). A blue background with yellow and white side mottling make this one of the most attractive rockfishes. It grows to only 30 to 43 cm (12 to 17 in.) and ranges from central California to south-eastern Alaska.

Quillback rockfish (Sebastes maliger). The white dorsal fin and very long dorsal spines of this species inspired its Latin name maliger *which translates as "mast-bearer." Quillback rockfish frequent inlets and shallow waters and are taken commercially to some extent. Individuals reach a length of 61 cm (24 in.) and range from central California to the Gulf of Alaska.*

The copper rockfish (Sebastes caurinus) is very common in shallow waters throughout British Columbia where it is fished commercially using hand lines and otter trawls. Mature length of the species is 55 cm (21 in.). Its full range extends from Monterey, California, to the Gulf of Alaska.

John E. Ketcheson

Pierre Dow

Painted greenling or convict fish (Oxylebius pictus). As this species almost never takes bait, it will seldom be encountered when fishing. During the breeding season, which may be six months of the year in the warmer waters of California and perhaps half that to the north, say, in Puget Sound, the males are highly territorial. A complete breeding cycle is approximately 30 days, depending on temperature and is repeated for as long as the season lasts. After a ripe female deposits her eggs within a male's territory, she departs, leaving the male to guard the eggs against predators until hatching.

The species grows to 25 cm (10 in.) and ranges over rocky areas from southern California to the Queen Charlotte Islands, British Columbia.

Pierre Dow

SHARKS, SKATES AND RAYS (CHONDRICHTHYS)

The old adage of a few bad apples spoiling the barrel is certainly applicable to the sharks. The fear and loathing the group inspires rests on the very undesirable behavior of a few. Of the approximately 280 species alive today, only a dozen or so are proven man-eaters, a number are considered threatening if provoked, and the rest are either too small or lack the kinds of jaws and teeth needed to inflict serious damage upon human swimmers. Contrary to popular belief, man-eating sharks do not deliberately seek out human prey but, like so many "opportunity feeders," will take whatever is available, people included. Shark behavior, particularly attacking behavior, is of a highly unpredictable nature. Attacks are not limited to a particular location, time, season or other condition. However, statistics indicate that sharks prefer to take human prey in waters warmer than 20° C. (68° F.). (Perhaps this is because more human bathers will occur at any one time in warmer water than in cold.) Yet even this generalization is not without exception. The great white shark (*Carcharodon carcharias*), most feared man-eater of all, has been known to attack swimmers in waters of 13° C. (55° F.). off the coast of California. This species is wide-ranging and is thought to prefer temperate waters. In 1968, the car-

cass of a 5-meter (16-foot) specimen was found on the the beach of Graham Island in the Queen Charlottes.

Only one problem species occurs with regularity in Pacific Northwest waters — the blue shark (*Prionace glauca*). Ranging from southern California to Alaska, the blue is not a proven man-eater but is listed as potentially dangerous.

Sharks are an ancient group and, in many respects, a primitive one. Along with the skates and rays, which are essentially very flattened sharks, they are separated from most other fishes by having a skeleton, not of bone but of cartilage. Hence the sharks, skates and rays are termed *cartilaginous fishes.* Unlike higher fishes, referred to as bony fishes, sharks and their relatives exhale water through multiple gill slits on either side of the head, as distinct from the single opening and cover plate (the operculum) in the bony fishes. Shark skin is not covered by the typical shingle-like scales of most other fishes, but has embedded in its surface minute spines giving the skin a very rough texture. These are known as denticles (*denticulus*, a "little tooth"), or *placoid scales.* Shark teeth are actually modified denticles and they grow in several rows in the upper and lower jaws, the front row being functional and the back rows being in reserve for constant replacement. However, not all sharks use their teeth as a means for capturing prey. Both the whale shark (*Rhineodon typus*) and the local 11-meter (36-foot) basking shark (*Cetorhinus maximus*) feed by straining plankton through sievelike structures on the gills known as gill-rakers. Water and plankton enter through the huge mouth. As the water passes over the gills, small organisms are retained on the inside of the gills, in the throat, and are swallowed.

Sharks do not spawn, that is, they do not release eggs and sperm into the water for fertilization. Rather the sharks and rays copulate, the eggs being fertilized within the body of the female. In all male sharks and rays the inner edge of the pelvic fins are modified to form an elongate clasper, an erectile organ used to

Tidepool sculpin (Oigocottus maculosus), as the common name suggests, is frequently found in tide pools of rocky shores. Color is variable from red-brown, red, or green on the upper (dorsal) surface and paler on the belly. The species grows to 8.9 cm (3.5 in.) and ranges from northern California to the Bering Sea. Observations of tidepool sculpins in aquaria indicate there may be some kind of copulation during spawning.

Staghorn sculpin (Leptocottus armatus). A large — to 46 cm (18 in.) — scaleless sculpin, this species is abundant in shallow and protected sandy areas. It tends to bury itself in the sand, leaving only its bulbous eyes exposed. The common name "staghorn" refers to the antler-like spine on the operculum (gill cover). Staghorn sculpins range from Baja California, to the Gulf of Alaska.

The grunt sculpin (Rhamphocottus richardsoni) is so named for the peculiar grunting noises it makes when removed from water. It pulls itself over rocky bottoms using finger-like pectoral fins. A long pointed snout pokes into crevices and between barnacles searching for small crustaceans and other organisms. Grunt sculpins grow to 7.6 cm (3 in.) and range from California to the Bering Sea.

The northern spearnose poacher (Agonopsis emmelane) is thought to be a nocturnal fish, foraging only at night. It grows to 20 cm (8 in.) and ranges from California to southeastern Alaska. It occurs subtidally, from the surface to 70 fathoms.

The red Irish lord (Hemilepidotus hemilepidotus) is predominantly red with spotting and mottling of brown, white and black. Adults feed on crabs, barnacles and mussels and are known to bury themselves in the sand. Red Irish lords grow to 51 cm (20 in.) and range from California to Alaska.

transfer sperm to the female during copulation. Eggs may be deposited in egg cases, as is the case with most skates. Within the egg case, commonly referred to as a "mermaid's purse," further development takes place, the young eventually emerging from the case as miniatures of the adult; or young may be born alive, as is the case with most sharks, the eggs having hatched and developed within the mother's uterus. In the spiny dogfish (*Squalus acanthias*) the time from copulation to birth is two years. At birth the pups are between 25 and 27.5 centimeters (10 to 11 inches), a good size considering the adult female is seldom more than 120 centimeters (4 feet) in length and males are smaller at just over 90 centimeters (3 feet). A single litter may range from two to seventeen young but seven or eight is most usual.

Because most newborn sharks enter the world in a fairly well-advanced state of development, fewer eggs are needed for survival of the species. This is in direct contrast to the herring, for example, which spawns thousands of free-floating pelagic eggs, exposed to all manner of physical disaster and predation from the very moment of fertilization.

Predators must be able to receive and interpret information from their environment quickly and accurately if they are to be effective hunters. Sharks are no exception. Vision, at least at close range, is good. Vibrations and pressure waves are perceived through the lateral line. Keenest of all is the sense of smell. A nose as we know it does not exist in the shark, rather there is a sac lined with sensory cells capable of responding to chemical "smells" in the water. Other small sensory sacs of the head region, known as the "ampullae of Lorenzi," provide information concerning salinity, pressure, temperature and electrical current. It is obvious that sharks are very much on top of what is going on within their world.

A species not infrequently taken in British Columbia in purse seines and on other fishing gear is the six-gill or mud shark (*Hexanchus griseus*). It is a sluggish, deep water species found in most temperate oceans of the world. The largest Pacific specimen recorded was 4.5 meters (15 feet) in length.

By far the most commonly encountered shark in the Pacific Northwest is the spiny dogfish. It ranges in the eastern Pacific from Baja California to the Bering Sea but is most abundant between northern California and northern British Columbia. Two long spines, one in front of each dorsal fin, and the relatively small size of the species (between 90 and 160 centimeters [3 and 5 feet]) readily distinguish the dogfish from other local sharks. Carelessness when handling dogfish, particularly when removing one from fishing gear, may result in a painful wound. On the back of each spine is a shallow groove containing venom. As the spine enters the victim's skin, the venom gland is damaged, releasing its fluid into the flesh.

Dogfish feed on a great variety of foods, principally herring, sand lance, smelt and shrimp. It is not surprising then that dogfish are attracted by the same bait and lures used in salmon-fishing, the salmon feeding on the same general diet. It is the general impression among sports fishermen that more dogfish occur in local waters than all other species put together. An exaggeration certainly, but the shark is abundant, and more so now than thirty years ago. This is in part due to the collapse of what was a substantial commercial fishery. In the late 1930s, dogfish were harvested for the high Vitamin A content of the livers. By 1950, liver oil imported from Japan and the advent of synthetic vitamins forced the fishery's closure. Combined with the fact that dogfish are no longer being harvested commercially, they are a very long-lived species — to forty years — in contrast to a fish such as the salmon with a life span of four to seven years.

If one is able to see past the dogfish as a scourge and look at it simply as another fish, it soon becomes apparent that in terms of design and motion the shark is near-perfection. It has a primitive body plan, little altered over the course of 200 million years, which serves the predator well.

A total of eleven species of shark occur in local waters. A few have already been mentioned and for a complete description of all species the reader is referred to J. L. Hart's *Pacific Fishes of Canada*, (Ottawa: Information Canada, 1973).

RATFISH

A most peculiar animal to see and to classify is the ratfish. It belongs somewhere between the sharks and bony fishes having sharklike characteristics: a cartilage skeleton, paired claspers in the male for internal fertilization, and eggs enclosed in horny capsules. Yet, like bony fishes, ratfish have a gill plate cover (operculum) and a more advanced jaw structure.

Ratfish propel themselves, not with the tail fin as do most fish, but with broad sweeps of the huge pectoral fins, like a bird flapping its wings. A disproportionately large head with rabbit-like teeth, huge

Wolf eel (Anarrhichthys ocellatus). No other fish is easily mistaken for this fierce-looking and powerful predator. Because it is a sluggish swimmer, wolf eels generally attack only slow-moving prey such as crustaceans, urchins, clams, mussels and the occasional slow-moving bottom fish. Male and female pairs often inhabit the same rocky den in shallow to moderately deep water from southern California to the Gulf of Alaska. The female, at least in captivity, is known to encircle the egg mass and maintain a water current over the eggs by undulating her long dorsal fin. The male wolf eel has a proportionately larger head and thicker lips than the female. Length is to 2.4 m (8 ft.).

Vancouver Sun Photo

144

The juvenile wolf eel is beautifully marked in tones of orange, gold and black. Mature wolf eels are generally dark blue-grey, with older specimens being much paler and often marked with many white lines in a kind of cross-hatching. The young specimen illustrated here was 30 cm (12 in.) long and probably a year old.

Wolf eel skull. Note the very well-developed canine teeth used for crushing shelled invertebrates such as clams and crabs. Strong crushing molars further back in the jaw grind food before it is swallowed. This skull was prepared from a 150 cm (5 ft.) specimen.

Finn Larsen

Ron Long

green eyes, long ratlike tail and a club-shaped process on the forehead of the male combine to create what can only be described as strange. The local species, *Hydrolagus colliei*, ranges from southern California to Alaska and is thought to be a nocturnal browser.

BONY FISHES (TELEOSTOMI)

Two-thirds of all living fish species are classed together as bony fishes (the *Teleostomi*) as opposed to the hagfish and lampreys (the *Agnatha*) and the sharks, skates and rays (the *Chondrichthys*). As would be expected, there exists within the class an enormous range of size, form and habitat. Bony fishes range in size from 1 centimeter ($\frac{1}{2}$ inch) to 4.58 meters (15 feet). Most fall within the 2.5-to-30-centimeter (1-to-12-inches) range

145

Tiger rockfish (Sebastes nigrocinctus). *The Greek and Latin names given to this species translate to "magnificent black belt," and a magnificent fish it is. Individuals are solitary, living in caves at depths of 30 to 50 fathoms. The tiger rockfish ranges from central California to southeast Alaska and grows to 60 cm (24 in.).*

Striped seaperch (Embiotoca lateralis) *possibly the most strikingly colored fish of the North Pacific region, with its bright copper ground and electric blue horizontal stripes. Like other seaperches, the young are born alive and fully formed. Mating is preceded by an elaborate courtship, with the males approaching the females on their sides and quivering rapidly. The anal fin is modified as a copulatory organ. The species grows to 38 cm (15 in.) and ranges from northern Baja California, to southeast Alaska.*

Adult yelloweye rockfish or red snapper (Sebastes ruber-rimus) is an excellent eating fish. Yelloweye rockfish are taken on set lines in relatively deep water. Adults are uniform red-orange whereas juveniles are deep maroon with wide horizontal white bands. For many years the two color phases were considered to denote different species. Adults reach a length of 90 cm (36 in.). The species is common in British Columbia and ranges from Baja California, to the Gulf of Alaska.

▼

Juvenile yelloweye rockfish or red snapper (Sebastes ruberrimus).

Pierre Dow

Pierre Dow

Male kelp greenling (Hexagrammos decagrammus). *The male kelp greenling is a very handsome fish and quite different in color and pattern from the rather drab female. At spawning time, males tend to concentrate much blue in the head region further adding to their already attractive appearance. The species ranges from southern California to southeastern Alaska along the west coast and is particularly common along the rocky shores of British Columbia.*

John F. Quail

and therefore exploit a smaller living space than the sharks, for example. Well-developed jaws, greater and more precise mobility, and a swim bladder have been responsible for much of this group's phenomenal success in the aquatic realm.

Bony fishes usually have true bone present in the skull, jaws or pectoral arch. There is one external gill opening covered by an operculum, and two sets of mobile paired fins, the pectorals (front or side pair) and pelvics (rear or ventral pair). Unlike the sharks, the bony fishes can twist, turn, spread, or flatten the fins allowing a much greater range and control of movement. The flexibility, yet rigidity, of bony fish fins is the result of rays and spines articulating on basal elements.

SALMON

Of the six species of Pacific salmon, five occur in the Pacific Northwest. (The Japanese cherry salmon (*Oncorhynchus masou*) is limited to the Japanese islands and nearby Asian mainland). The different species vary in size, habits, life span and spawning time, yet all share a similar life history. The salmon begin life in fresh water, migrate to the sea and reach maturity there. As spawning time approaches, adults return to the fresh-water streams of their birth to spawn and then die. Fishes such as the Pacific lamprey and salmon, which return to fresh waters to spawn, are known as *anadromous* fishes.

The Pacific salmon are all of the same genus, *Onchorhynchus*, and are distinct from the Atlantic species, though it is thought that the Atlantic and Pacific species arose from a common ancestor which ranged both oceans until Arctic ice blocked passage between the two seas some two million years ago.

The salmons are sleek and beautiful creatures. They are prized sports fish, delicious eating and the basis of a 400,000-ton annual fishery in Canada.

148

*Female kelp greenling (**Hexagrammos decagrammus**). The female of the species is pale in comparison to the male. Kelp greenlings, like their cousins the lingcod, are voracious feeders and have been reported to eat almost anything including anemones. Adults attain a length of 53 cm (21 in.).*

*Lingcod (**Ophiodon elongatus**) are not cod at all but belong to the greenling family. They occur from Baja, California, to Alaska in shallow water and to depths of 230 fathoms in the southern part of their range, and generally within the upper 50 fathoms in British Columbia. Females grow faster and larger than males. A very large male seldom exceeds 11.5 kg (25 lb.), whereas females have been recorded in excess of 45 kg (100 lb.). Toward the end of November in British Columbia the male establishes within his territory a site where the female will lay her eggs. After the eggs are laid in December, the female departs, leaving the male to guard the egg mass until hatching in March.*

Lingcod are fished commercially for the fresh fish trade, particularly for use in making high-quality fish and chips.

The silverspotted sculpin (Blepsias cirrhosus) is so named for the chrome-silver spot just back of the pectoral fins. In the adult the spot becomes very pronounced to a slash of silver. The silverspotted sculpin inhabits weedy shallows and kelp beds both on exposed shores and in more protected waters. When swimming, the pectorial fins are extended like an airplane's wings, with the rippling dorsal fin providing propulsion. The species grows to 19 cm (7.5 in.) and ranges from northern California to the Bering Sea.

The C-O sole (Pleuronichthys coenosus) is dark brown on its upper surface and bears a distinct black spot in the middle. It grows to 36 cm (14 in.) and ranges from Baja California, to Alaska. Juveniles frequent shallow inshore waters; adults occur to 190 fathoms. The species gets its common name from the "C" and "O" markings on the tail. It is frequently referred to as "the popeye" by fishermen.

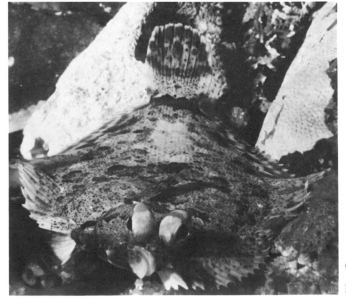

The rockhead or pitted poacher (Bothragonus swanii) may be brown, orange or red with dark bars. It takes one of its common names from the deep cavity on the top of the head; the exact function of the cavity is not known. The species grows to 8.9 cm (3.5 in.) and ranges from northern California to Alaska. They are infrequently seen in tidepools of exposed coasts.

Pierre Dow

The starry flounder (Platichthys stellatus) is a very common flatfish of shallow water and is easily distinguished by alternate dark and light bars on the dorsal and anal fins (side fins in the flatfishes). Though they grow to a good size, 91 cm (3 ft.) and 9.1 kg (20 lb.), they are not highly regarded commercially. Starry flounders, particularly juveniles, make their way into brackish water areas at river mouths.

Pacific halibut (Hypoglossus stenolepis). The halibut illustrated here was over 880 kg (400 lb.) before head and entrails were removed. It is the largest taken in recent years off the coast of British Columbia; a larger, 888.8 kg (404 lb.) fish (dressed weight), was taken from the same area off the Queen Charlotte Islands in 1914. The specimen shown here was taken on a 12 mile long set line with hooks at eighteen foot intervals.

Female halibut are typically larger than males with maximum recorded dressed weights of 216 kg (475 lb.) for females and 56 kg (123 lb.) for males. These are records, however, and most are proportionately smaller. Unlike most flatfishes, which are sedentary bottom dwellers, halibut are fast-moving, active predators feeding voraciously on other fish. When taken on hook and line the halibut is a formidable fighting fish.

Vancouver Sun Photo

region. Rockfish of the genus *Sebastes* are ovoviviparous, meaning the eggs are retained and develop within the female's body and the larvae are born alive. Rockfish of the genus *Sebastolobus* are oviparous, meaning they lay eggs and do not give birth to live young.

All rockfish are edible, some are delicious table fish, and a number of species are fished commercially with trawls, hook and line, or gill nets.

Rockfish occur from shallow water to depths of 430 fathoms and are primarily bottom-dwelling fish. The large mobile fins and swim bladder afford them great mobility and stability in confined rocky areas where non-schooling species establish themselves in rocks and crevices.

The rockfishes are opportunity feeders taking smaller fish, crustaceans, tunicates, jellyfish and squid. It must be mentioned that the name "rockcod" is a misnomer as the rockfish are in no way related to the codfish.

SCULPINS (COTTIDAE)

This is a large group of fishes (some 300 species) occurring in a great variety of forms. Most are bottom dwellers of shallow waters. Sculpins are characterized by stout forward bodies tapering off to a much slimmer posterior portion. Eyes are usually large and positioned high on the head. Pectoral fins are typically fan-shaped and large with the pelvic fins positioned far forward.

POACHERS (AGONIDAE)

Poachers are generally small bottom fishes living at moderate depths. Some occur in deep water, a few in tide pools. The body is covered with bony plates which meet but do not overlap.

FLATFISHES

Twenty-one different species of flatfishes occur off the British Columbia coast. These are popularly termed *sole, halibut* and *flounder*. Most are bottom fishes, frequently in very deep water.

ROCKFISH (SCORPAENIDAE)

There are more species of rockfish in the Pacific Northwest than any other fish family. In California, fifty-three species have been recorded, in British Columbia, thirty-five species. The family, *Scorpaenidae*, is a large one.

Rockfish are distinguished by having eleven to seventeen long, heavy spines in the dorsal fin but lack the venom gland of their notorious cousin, the Indo-Pacific stonefish. The mouth and eyes are large and many smaller spines occur on the head and gill cover

Sea Mammals

Sea Otters, Seals, Sea Lions, Whales and Dolphins

SEA OTTERS

"Such is the beauty of the animal and especially of its skin that this otter is alone and without equal, for in the amazing beauty and softness of its fur it surpasses all other creatures of the vast ocean."

G. W. Steller,* 1751

In 1741, an expedition headed by Vitus Bering, a Danish explorer in the service of Russia, discovered the home of the sea otter in the Aleutian Islands. This newfound knowledge spurred a relentless hunt which was to last 170 years in response to the Chinese and Russian fur markets. The Siberians plundered island after island, slaughtering the sea otter, until they reached the North American continent in a continuing search for the coveted fur.

By the end of the eighteenth century, otter herds in the western and central Aleutians had greatly diminished, causing these interesting creatures to change their way of life. Only the most violent storms could drive them to the beaches where they had once slept and given birth. They now spent their whole lives in the sea.

Captain James Cook's crew traded trinkets for sea otter pelts with the Nootka Indians. When the skins reached China, the prices received were enough to launch the English into the sea otter trade, breaking the Russian monopoly. Adventurers from European countries and, later, Americans were quick to join the highly profitable enterprise which led to the near-extinction of the sea otter.

Finally, in 1911, the United States, Great Britain, Russia and Japan signed a treaty making it illegal to kill a sea otter or to possess a pelt. This treaty was primarily for the protection of the fur seal, the sea otter being secondarily included though they were thought to be extinct. Fortunately, some animals had survived in a few secluded bays in the Aleutians, the Kuril Islands, Alaska, British Columbia and California, and very slowly their numbers increased (except in British Columbia where they died out).

The sea otter (*Enhydra lutris*) is the smallest and least specialized of the marine mammals, a true marine mammal being one which makes its living exclusively from the sea. It is not related to whales, seals and sea lions, but is the largest member of the family *Mustelidae*; a family which includes skunks, weasels, badgers, minks and river otters. Unlike its cousins, however, the sea otter does not possess anal scent glands.

Because they are both often seen swimming in coastal waters, sea otters are frequently confused with river otters (*Lutra canadensis*). Both species are approximately the same length, 127 centimeters (50 inches), but in proportion to its length the sea otter is a heavier-bodied animal. Its tail is shorter and flattened, its hind feet are webbed, its cheek bristles are very long and mustache-like and it has the habit of swimming on its back. When on land, sea otters are rather clumsy, while river otters are agile and have land-oriented limbs.

Although river otters are seen swimming in coastal waters, they are seldom found far from a source of fresh water and habitually "den-up" on land at night and to have their young. This is not the case with sea otters which spend the majority of their time in the water except in remote northern regions where they may occasionally come up on land to sleep. Sea otters do not prepare a land-based den in which to produce and care for young.

The sea otter has little blubber, or fat layer, for insulation. How, then, does this creature maintain its body warmth in the chill waters it inhabits? To combat the cold, the sea otter has developed a pelt dense enough to provide a warm, dry blanket against its skin. The thick, fine, brown fur of the sea otter is twice as dense (100,800 hairs to the square centimeter) as the next most densely pelaged mammal, the fur seal. This fine hair traps a layer of air next to the skin, providing

* Georg Wilhelm Steller, a German naturalist, accompanied Bering on his expedition to Alaska.

*The river otter (*Lutra canadensis *is very much at home in the coastal marine environment and the offshore archipelagos. Consequently it is frequently mistaken for its somewhat longer and more heavy bodied cousin, the sea otter. The river otter is not a true marine mammal like the sea otter, and must return to land to sleep, mate and bear and rear its young.*

warmth and buoyancy and allowing the sea otter to float easily at the water's surface. If the fur becomes soiled, the waterproofing and insulating quality of the fur is lost and the animal quickly dies of cold and exposure. Because of this, sea otters spend a great deal of time "grooming" their fur in order to keep it clean. This involves vigorous scrubbing of the entire body with their handlike forepaws while blowing air into the fur. Rolling and somersaulting during the grooming flushes away debris and smoothes the outer guard hairs. Because the sea otter is dependent on the condition of its fur for survival, this animal is extremely sensitive to water pollution. Ironically, this luxuriant fur was the reason for its near-extinction a hundred years ago.

Even with its magnificent pelt, the sea otter has a high metabolic rate to help keep it warm. This requires an enormous amount of food, each individual consuming 20 to 25 percent of its body weight each day. Thus, an average male of 30 kilograms (65 pounds) would eat 7.2 kilograms (16 pounds) of food daily. Sea otters are constantly eating, their diet consisting of molluscs, sea urchins, crabs, worms, shrimp, tunicates and fish. To get at these items the sea otter makes short dives of 15.25 to 30.5 meters (50 to 100 feet) collecting the food in pouchlike flaps of loose skin between the forelegs and body. Returning to the surface with its bounty, the otter rolls on its back, using its chest as a kind of lunch counter. When the meal is finished, vigorous scrubbing and rolling provide the cleanup.

Sea otters living off California show a most interesting behavior pattern when feeding. Floating on its back, an individual may place a stone (or clam shell) on its chest and then proceed to pound a clam or sea urchin against the stone. Interestingly, this "tool-using" activity is seldom seen in northern populations. Behaviorists do not consider this an intelligent ability to anticipate a need for a tool, but merely an instinctive response.

Mating occurs in water, and one offspring is born every other year after a gestation period of approximately nine months. The 1.9-to-2.3-kilogram (4-to-5-pound) pup is usually born on land and is fully developed, but helpless. Female sea otters do not have a den for their young, but the mother cradles the pup on her chest as she swims on her back. Observations of wild sea otters indicate not only that there is a long period of dependency (approximately one year), but also that the female otter is unusually solicitous and protective of her young. She will swim on her back, holding the pup on her chest where it nurses at her abdominal nipples. If danger threatens, she will take the pup in

*Sea otter (*Enhydra lutris*).*

Peter Hulbert, Vancouver Province

her forepaws and dive underwater. She continually licks, combs and washes the young animal, leaving it only when she is getting food. At such times, the pup is left floating on its back while she dives. On land, the mother may rest on her back with the pup on her chest, and should she move around, the pup hangs onto its mother by the teeth, dangling like a limp bag.

Diurnal (daytime) in their habits, sea otters congregate in groups of about thirty animals, known as *rafts*. They are known to segregate into "male" and "female" areas, in the water and on land. While most activities take place in the water (eating, grooming, dozing, mating and play), sea otters do occasionally haul out on land to dry their fur and sleep. When dozing in the water, otters are known to wrap themselves in kelp to keep from drifting.

Sea otters make a variety of sounds: they scream when distressed, coo when mating or fondling young, whistle when frustrated, snarl when captured, grunt when eating and bark when cornered.

Natural repopulation of areas where the sea otter once flourished has been very slow. Wide expanses of ocean where the animal can obtain little food or shelter hinder migrations to new territories. The natural ecological zone of the sea otter is a narrow one. It is an area close to a coastline or island sheltered

155

from wind and storm waves, with an abundant invertebrate fauna for food. While many such areas exist, it is almost impossible for the sea otter to reach them without help. To facilitate repopulation of certain areas, various government agencies have tried transplants. A transplant involves capturing animals in an established area and conveying them to another area that once had otters and is considered suitable. Attempts have been made to repopulate the outer coasts of Oregon, Washington, British Columbia and southeastern Alaska with sea otters from the more northerly Alaska populations. However, it will be several years before biologists can evaluate the success of these endeavors.

Today one can only imagine what the large aggregations of sea otters looked like to the explorers as they traveled up the North Pacific coast. Interwoven with the search for the Northwest Passage and discovery of the North Pacific, the sea otter and its history are an important chapter in our natural heritage.

SEALS AND SEA LIONS

Coastal peoples have long known and utilized the sea dogs or seals. We know this from drawings of these animals found on pieces of reindeer antler dated from Paleolithic times, from references to seals in works of the classical Greek poets and writers, and from many ancient beliefs. For example, a seal flipper under the pillow was considered to be a cure for insomnia and sealskin garments were thought to protect the wearer from lightning strikes. Today, seal liver remains a source of Vitamin A for many northern Eskimos in a land where fresh vegetables are not available.

The seals have replaced the walking limbs with flippers more efficient for swimming. Sea dogs are the *pinnipeds*; from the Latin *pinna*, "feather" and *pedes*, "feet." True marine mammals, like the sea otter and the whales, the pinnipeds derive their sole living from the sea. Seals seek their food at depths to 600 meters (1968 ft), and are able to remain underwater for

five to twenty minutes. As an adaptation for capturing prey, the seals and sea lions have very large eyes, capable of appreciating extremely low light levels in the darker depths. At least one pinniped, the California sea lion, is known to possess a degree of echolocation, an obvious advantage in deep water fishing. During a dive the metabolic rate falls, the heart beat slows to as low as one-tenth the normal, body temperature drops, and there is *peripheral vasoconstriction.* This means that normal blood flow is greatly reduced to all but the essential organs, such as the heart and brain. These physiological changes conserve vital oxygen during the dive when the animal is without air. So well adapted are the pinnipeds to their life in the sea that they retain only one link with the land of their progenitors; they must return to land for the birth of their young.

Pinnipeds have been classed in three families; the walrus (*Odobenidae*), the fur seal and sea lion (*Otariidae*), and the true, or earless, seal (*Phocidae*). In total, forty-seven different kinds (thirty-one species, sixteen subspecies) make up a world population of perhaps fifteen to twenty-five million individuals. These are found in the Arctic and Antarctic Oceans and adjacent cooler waters. Where seals have extended their ranges to more temperate or tropical areas, these can generally be found to follow quite closely the cold ocean currents to such places as Hawaii, Australia, New Zealand and the Galapagos Islands.

The well-known circus seal, performing feats of balance and precision, applauding its own performance with long front flippers is, in fact, a California sea lion. It is distinguished from the true seal by having small ear pinnae and very long hairless flippers which can support its body upright on land. The hind flippers can be rotated forward enabling the sea lions and fur seals to move at a fast gallop. The true seal is a plump, fusiform (tapering) animal with short, furred flippers and could not possibly manage the feats of a sea lion. It has a round, smooth head with no external

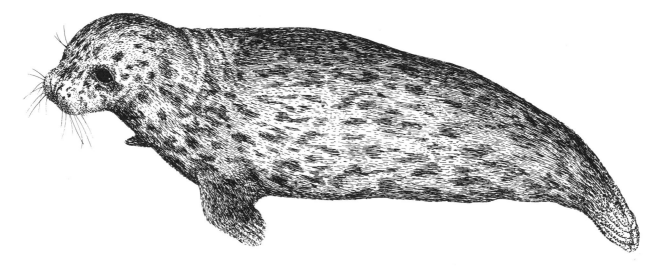

*An "earless seal," the harbor seal (*Phoca vitulina*).*

ears, hence the name "earless seal."

The most common true seal of the Pacific Northwest is the harbor seal (*Phoca vitulina*), found in bays and inlets from China to the Bering Sea and south to Baja California. Harbor seals grow to 114 kilograms (250 pounds) and 156 to 187 centimeters (5 to 6 feet) in length. They swim using a sculling motion of the hind flippers, the short tail tucked neatly between them. On the water they are recognized by the manner in which they approach the surface for air, rising from directly beneath the surface and hanging vertically in the water while surveying their surroundings. Because they are unable to rotate their hind flippers forward, they move on land in a caterpillar-like motion, using the front flippers to pull themselves forward, the hind flippers dragging, or held aloft. Lacking swift mobility on land, true seals like the harbor seal, seldom haul out more than a few yards from shore and easy escape from land predators. Although they are able to sleep comfortably in the water, these seals generally haul out to sleep and to enjoy the benefits of dryness and sunshine for a good part of the day.

The harbor seal mates about September, usually in the water though sometimes on land, especially on sandbars. The resultant young are born in spring or early summer on a secluded sandbar or beach. Pups are between 8 to 11.3 kilograms (18 to 25 pounds) at birth, fully furred and able to swim. Pups born in the southern areas of their range bear the same brown, tan and black mottled fur pattern as the adults, whereas those born in the northern areas retain for a short period a white fetal coat, an adaptation to early life in a land of snow and ice. Harbor seals are gentle and devoted mothers, playing swimming games with their young and responding quickly to their human-sounding cry. A mother may leave her young momentarily to feed, or if disturbed, but soon returns to retrieve her pup. A well-meaning person should make absolutely certain, by retreating to a distance and watching for the return of the mother, that a pup is truly abandoned before taking steps to take and care for it.

The nursing period for harbor seals is short, four to six weeks, by which time the pup has a good set of sharp teeth and is weaned to an adult diet of fish, molluscs and crustaceans.

Just as the true seals and eared seals differ physically, so they exhibit markedly different breeding behavior. The true seals, like the harbor seal, are

157

The harbor seal (Phoca vitulina) *is a common, inshore and year-round resident of both coasts of North America. They are often seen hauled out on sandbars and secluded beaches. A single 10-kg (20-lb.) pup is born in June or July. Unlike the Steller's sea lion pup which may nurse for up to a year, the young harbor seal is weaned by six weeks of age.*

promiscuous, whereas the eared seals, like the Steller sea lion (*Eumetopias jubata*) of the Pacific Northwest, have what is known as a "harem" system. This breeding behavior results in a distinct, annual, social and biological ritual. The center of activity is the rookery; in this case, exposed rocky islands off the west coast of British Columbia — Cape Scott Island and Cape St. James, the Queen Charlotte Islands.

The phenomenon begins with the arrival of breeding males in early spring. These are enormous buff-colored animals, largest of the eared seals, up to 3.05 meters (10 feet) in length and weighing in excess of a ton. The battles for territories begin as the largest and strongest, usually those of about twelve years of age, establish areas of their own. This area, known as a "territory," is approximately 55 meters (600 feet) square, depending on the physical characteristics of the land. Only those bulls which gain a territory will have access to the females. The younger males, while sexually mature, may be unable to compete for a territory and must retreat to another area known as a "bachelor island." Much of the confrontation occurring between males is bluff, noise and posture. However, if one male puts any part of his body into an-

A young Steller's sea lion "tanking-up" (nursing). The mother may go to sea for several days to feed before again returning to nurse her young.

Hans Meyer

other's territory, the defender is bound to attack his opponent with a vicious lunge at the neck, using his powerful teeth. The great neck mane and blubber of the huge males is of obvious survival value in battle.

In June and July the females arrive, establishing themselves in an acceptable area. They are much smaller than the males, 228 centimeters (7½ feet) in length and weighing up to 454 kilograms (1,000 pounds). This difference in size is referred to as sexual dimorphism.

It was previously thought that the harem bull, a male having a territory, chose and fought over specific females. It is now known that he simply provides housing, so to speak, the females moving freely between territories, often pupping in one, mating in

another, and nursing in yet another.

Within a few hours or days the newly arrived females will give birth to a single pup, the offspring of the previous year's mating. After a two-week period of frequent nursing, she will come into estrus, or heat, and be mated for the following year by the bull whose territory she is in.

But even residence by females is no guarantee of success for the battle-worn males. One intrepid biologist, studying Steller sea lion-breeding behavior, has this story to tell:

Prior to the arrival of the males on the rookery, an observation blind was constructed on the windswept island. True to nature, the bulls arrived and began contesting for territories. One large, but younger, bull

managed to establish a very small territory, hardly much larger than himself, near the water's edge. For this the young gallant was prepared to fight to the death. On schedule the females arrived and not one took up residence on the small rock by the sea. However, as the females began giving birth and nursing, they soon established a routine of leaving the larger territories in order to feed at sea, returning between trips to suckle their young. Many females had to pass the seaside rock occupied by the lone bull, and many were eventually serviced by him as they came and went. The bull with the most females on his territory ended up with only the noise and congestion of mothers and pups without the benefit of any love making to make it all worthwhile.

Female Steller sea lions are, at best, indifferent mothers, doing little else than nurse their young on very rich milk. Seal milk is composed of 42 percent fat, compared to human mothers' milk at 2 to 3 percent fat. The richness of the milk guarantees a rapid growth rate and a fast accumulation of a blubber layer; this layer adds buoyancy, insulates against cold, provides streamlining, and serves as an energy reserve. The growth rate of all seals is enormous, and, for some, phenomenal. For example, the southern elephant seal which is 45.5 kilograms (100 pounds) at birth, quadruples its weight in three weeks, while harbor seal pups double their weight during the same period.

The young Steller sea lion learns to swim on its own at about three weeks of age, in the now fetid tide pools on the rookery. Sea lions do not involve themselves with any sanitary considerations and, over the weeks on the rookery, wastes accumulate to such an extent it is perhaps fortunate that the sea lions have a poor sense of smell. At the age of three months, those pups which have survived the rigors of rookery life are ready to go to sea and learn to catch fish, though they will continue nursing until nine months of age or longer.

By August, the function of the males on the rookery is complete and they depart. Most have not eaten during the three-month season but have lived off their blubber and must now replenish their body stores in preparation for winter. The females follow within a few months, ending the complex, but temporary, society of life on the rookery.

Often confused with the Steller sea lion is the California sea lion (*Zalophus californianus*). This species is much like the former in physical appearance and behavior but is smaller, darker in color (russet to brown) and more southern in its distribution (Mexico to southern California, with a winter range extending northward into British Columbia). The male California sea lion may reach 244 centimeters (8 feet) and 363 kilograms (800 pounds), with the female much smaller at 152.5 centimeters (5 feet) and 113 kilograms (250 pounds). Like the Steller, the California sea lion engages in the same kind of seasonal breeding behavior.

An occasional visitor to the Pacific Northwest is the northern fur seal (*Callorhinus ursinus*). It is the most truly oceanic of the North Pacific seals, ranging across the subarctic waters of the North Pacific Ocean, Bering and Okhotsk Seas, and into the Sea of Japan. It rarely comes ashore except on its home islands in the Pribilofs during the breeding season from May through October. After the breeding season, females and young depart from the north for the warmer waters of Japan and California. It is during their passage south in the fall and north in the spring that they may be seen off Oregon, Washington and British Columbia. The males remain in the northern waters of the Bering Sea and the Gulf of Alaska. Both sexes spend up to nine months at sea, the females and young travelling 9,600 to 12,600 kilometers (6,000 to 9,000 miles) during a single migration.

Called "fur seal" because of its very dense, dark fur with over 300,000 hairs to the square inch, this animal was once the object of massive commercial exploitation. During the period of Russian ownership

California sea lions (Zalophus californianus).

of the Pribilof Islands, it is estimated that 2.5 million skins were taken between 1786-1867. Large numbers were again taken when these islands became the property of the United States in 1867. The North Pacific Fur Seal Convention of 1911 now prohibits pelagic sealing except by aboriginal peoples using primitive methods. The taking of skins on land continues, but is regulated according to a sustained yield basis by member countries of the convention: Canada, Japan, Russia and the United States of America.

A relative newcomer to Pacific Northwest pinnipeds is the elephant seal (*Mirounga angustirostris*) —

an enormous animal. What this phocid lacks in beauty, it more than makes up for in size. The male weighs up to three tons and exceeds 5.5 meters (18 feet) in length. Females are smaller, at one ton, and measure 3.05 to 3.6 meters (10 to 12 feet). Like the land-living elephants, they are relatively hairless. The males of this species develop a strange proboscis, reminiscent of the trunk of the land elephant. This bulbous snout is inflated during courtship battles and, when relaxed, it hangs drooping over the mouth. This mammoth animal generally breeds in the warmer climes of southern California and Mexico, and the

bulls are infrequently seen in British Columbia waters. Unlike the other members of the true seal family (except for the grey seal of the Atlantic), the elephant seal has a kind of harem system, breeding in January and February on rookeries in southern California and Mexico. Again, unlike other phocids, the young cannot swim at birth, taking to the water at two months of age.

Like the northern fur seal, the elephant seal was the object of commercial sealing to such an extent that by 1900 it was thought extinct. The animal was taken not for its fur, but for its blubber; an average 3.6-meter (12-foot) bull yielding about 410 liters (90 gallons) of oil. The sealing which began in 1818 was no longer profitable by 1860, so extensive was the kill. In 1922, the Mexican government granted the elephant seal absolute protection.

In the United States protection has been granted to all marine mammals, including seals, under the Marine Mammal Protection Act of 1972. Basically, this Act states that it is illegal to take, hold, harass, or kill for any purpose any marine mammal, or tissues thereof, without a permit. In Canada, it is illegal to take, catch, kill, molest, disturb or be in possession of

Clumsy on land and an easy prey for hunters, the northern fur seal is streamlined and graceful under water.

an elephant seal or sea lion without a permit, except where a seal is causing damage to fish, nets or gear associated with those who earn their living by fishing. This protection is also extended to sea otters and killer whales.

Legislation can provide a seal or sea lion some degree of protection from man, but not from their natural enemies. The greatest single killer of pinnipeds is infestation by the small parasite, the nematode. This creature is responsible for at least 22 percent of fur seal pup mortality. Tapeworms, hook worms, nasal mites and lice are other common parasites which, while they may not kill the animals directly, weaken them to a degree where normal predator avoidance is impossible. Heaviest mortalities from all causes occur in the juvenile animals, the pups of many species falling prey to leopard seals, walruses, polar bears and

bald eagles. The greatest enemy of the adult seal is the killer whale in cooler waters, and large sharks in temperate and warmer seas.

WHALES AND DOLPHINS
Surrounded by myth and mystery, the whales and dolphins exist in complete harmony with their aquatic environment. They are mammals: warm-blooded, air breathing, successful through extreme adaptation to life in the water, and from birth until death, totally independent of the land. They are called *cetaceans.*

Cetaceans bear small resemblance to their land-dwelling ancestors. Just why a mammal would return to the sea and to the problems of mammalian existence in the water is not known. Perhaps it was in response to the need for more space, or a new food source, or to escape predation. One can only wonder.

164

Elephant Seal (Mirounga angustirostris).

C. Farwell

The cetaceans are divided into two groups on the basis of their very different feeding patterns. Most of the smaller whales and dolphins and porpoises are "toothed whales," or odontocetes. (There is, however, one large toothed whale, the sperm whale — the male growing to 18.3 meters (60 feet) and the female to 10.68 or 12.2 meters [35 or 40 feet]). As the name implies, these cetaceans have teeth, uniform in size and shape. They feed on fish and invertebrates such as squid and crustaceans. In the case of the killer whale, the diet is more varied and includes seabirds and marine mammals.

The larger whales belong to the group known as the *baleen whales*, or mysticetes. In this group, the teeth have been replaced with large structures called baleen. These plates of horny material hang like vertical venetian blinds from the upper jaw. They number 200 to 400 per side and are frayed into bristles on their inner edges. These elaborate structures are used to capture plankton or *krill*.

Plankton, found in the upper layers of the ocean, ranges from microscopic larval forms to small shrimps a few centimeters in size. It serves as a primary food source for the baleen whales, as well as a host of other marine animals.

In order to trap its food, a baleen whale swims through the plankton-rich sea, mouth open, engulfing plankton and sea water by the ton. By shutting its cavernous mouth and pressing its tongue against the back of the baleen bristles, it forces the water out of its mouth, trapping the plankton on a mat of overlapping baleen. It is by using a primary food source that the baleen whale is able to secure the enormous amounts of energy required to sustain its sometimes

165

huge body.

The largest animal ever to have lived on earth, larger by far than any dinosaur, is a baleen whale, the blue whale. This leviathan has been measured up to 30.5 meters (100 feet) in length with a corresponding weight of over 100 tons. The great size of this and other whales has been possible because they are suspended in water and do not have to support their weight on limbs against the pull of gravity, as do land animals.

One might well ask how a whale (or dolphin), an air-breather, is able to swim underwater with its mouth open and never run the risk of flooding its lungs. The answer? The "goosebeak larynx" leads air from the "blowhole," across the mouth cavity into the trachea. While land mammals are able to breath equally well through both nose and mouth, cetaceans have access to air only by way of a modified nostril, or blowhole, on the top of the head. A series of muscles surround this blowhole sealing its entrance when the animal submerges.

Cetaceans do not spout water. The visible spout, the size and shape of which is unique to many species, results from condensation of warm vapor entering the air from the lungs as the animal exhales. The spout effect is a result of rapid and forced exhalation of water vapor and a small amount of water present in the depression around the blowhole. Cetaceans do not breathe in the rhythmic, involuntary fashion of land mammals but inhale and exhale according to conscious effort, quickly and with force, literally blowing air from the lungs.

Unlike the baleen whales which feed near the water's surface, some toothed whales and dolphins dive to great depths in search of food. For example, the sperm whale is known to dive down 1.21 kilometers ($\frac{3}{4}$ mile) in search of its favorite prey, the giant squid. Consider that once this whale has left the air-water interface, it must make a mile-and-a-half round trip without breathing. How is this possible?

It is known that cetaceans have a larger blood volume than land mammals of comparable size and weight and that they have a greatly increased capacity to store oxygen in their blood and muscle tissue. In addition, they have a more efficient system of supplying oxygen to the blood: each breath provides an 80 to 90 percent renewal of air in the cetacean lung, compared to a renewal percentage of only 10 to 20 percent in most land mammals. Yet another important adaptation for prolonged breath-holding in cetaceans is their resistance to the metabolic by-product, carbon dioxide.

Contrary to what is commonly thought, it is the buildup of carbon dioxide in the tissues, not lack of oxygen, which triggers the involuntary breathing response of most mammals. Because the cetaceans have a high tolerance to carbon dioxide, they are able to remain submerged for longer periods without being overcome by the need to breathe. Even with all this, the cetaceans must "pant" at the surface to replenish their oxygen supply after a long period of submersion, in much the same way as a sprinter pants at the end of a race.

While the cetaceans' physiological mechanisms for coping with great pressure are far too technical to go into here, it is worth considering the weight of the water during a deep dive. For every ten meters in depth, the pressure increases at the rate of one "atmosphere," or 760 torr (1 millimeter of mercury [14.7 pounds per square inch]). The pressure exerted at 500 meters (1,640 feet) would be very great indeed.

At first glance, whales and dolphins appear remarkably fishlike. In truth, they are as far removed from fish as are human beings. Although the cetacean body has become exceedingly streamlined, it is based on mammalian structure. The front limbs have become modified as paddle-shaped flippers, the bones of which are reminiscent of jointed limbs and digits. The hind limbs have been lost, the bones of the pelvic girdle now serving only as anchors for the genital organs. The tail flukes which provide the main propul-

Killer whales (Orcinus orca) may attain bursts of speed to 25 m.p.h. They often hunt in packs like wolves, using their 44 to 50 sharp, conical teeth to tear flesh from seals, sea lions and even other whales. In the wild these whales are often heard before they are seen — the noise of their blowing and breaching carries for miles.

Finn Larsen

sive thrust of these creatures bear no anatomical connection to hind limbs, but are a separate and distinct development. The flukes, therefore, contain no bone, owing their firm, yet flexible shape to underlying fibrous and elastic tissue.

In order to provide a fluid, fusiform shape offering the least resistance while moving through water, the internal organs, skeleton and muscles are enclosed in a thick layer of blubber, smoothing and rounding out physical irregularities. The skin is modified as well, free of sweat glands, oil glands and hair (except for a few facial bristles in some species), and feels much like smooth, wet rubber to the touch.

Possibly the most fascinating aspect of whales and dolphins is not their extraordinary physical adaptations and capabilities, but their non-physical ones. Theirs is a world perceived largely through sound. Sound and hearing are to the whales and dolphins what vision is to most land mammals.

For years scientists have been intrigued by the ability of cetaceans to explore their environment and the objects in it through the use of echolocation. By directing sounds produced in the head region toward an object and receiving back the sound waves which bounce off the object, very fine discriminations can be made as to size, density, distance, and so on. The sound

waves are received as pulses through the lower jaw and transmitted to the inner ear. Because the sound waves are waterborne, cetaceans have been able to discard the structures which land mammals developed to gather airborne sounds, namely the external ear.

This system of sensing the environment is obviously of enormous advantage in orienting, navigating and capturing prey in dark or turbid waters. In essence, it is a means of scanning by sound for the same information we perceive by vision. This is not to say that cetaceans have poor sight. Researchers at the Vancouver Aquarium found that the visual acuity of the killer whale underwater was equal to that of a cat on land.

To whales and dolphins, sound communicates much of what other animals communicate through scent, posture and expression. Cetaceans lack any sense of smell. You will never see a whale curl its lips in a snarl or wag its tail. A female will not emit a distinctive scent, indicating a readiness to mate. In cetaceans these important messages are relayed, as they must be within a social group, by sound. It has been observed that female dolphins with young in captivity maintain almost constant vocal contact.

Because whales and dolphins are almost impossible to observe in their natural state, little is known of their social interaction in terms of communication and behavior in the wild. Some species exist, for the most part, as solitary animals. How do they locate a mate? Other species occur in pods numbering from a few animals to hundreds of individuals. How are they organized? Many details of cetacean behavior remain a mystery, yet there is one area of social behavior we know for a fact to be common to them all, and that is the pairing and ultimate mating between individuals of the species.

Brief mating occurs in the water. The pregnant female carries her unborn calf for eleven to sixteen months, depending on the species. As parturition approaches, she seeks out a sheltered area and gives birth

Pacific striped dolphin (Lagenorhynchus obliquidens). *Ranging from California north and across the Aleutian chain to Japan, this species travels in very large aggregations of up to 2,000 individuals. As illustrated here, the dolphin is pursuing one of its major food items, the herring. Many needle-sharp teeth grasp prey which is not chewed but swallowed whole.*

to a single calf, one-quarter to one-third her own length. The calf is born tail first and swims immediately, guided by its mother to the surface for its first breath. For up to two years, the calf will be nursed on rich mother's milk from two mammary teats enclosed in slits located on either side of the genital opening.

The mother-young bond is a strong one. The whalers, like the sea otter-hunters, capitalized on this strong attachment, capturing or killing the slower and weaker young in order to secure the adult, knowing that a mother would not leave her calf.

Because cetaceans breed slowly, producing only one offspring every two or three years, many have not been able to withstand the pressures of modern commercial whaling. Even in an undisturbed state, all young are not destined to reach adulthood. Disease, predators and natural disasters maintain an ecological balance in the wild as safeguards against overpopulation. Relentless hunting by high-speed whaling vessels equipped with explosive weapons in pursuit of animals that cannot run and cannot hide makes obvious the reason for there being few whales of some species now, where formerly there were many. The situation, however, is changing. For some it is too late; for others, such as the California Gray whale (*Eschrichtius glaucus*), uncontrolled commercial whaling was stopped in time.

The relatively slow swimming speed of the California Gray whale (4 to 5 knots cruising speed) and predictable seasonal migration routes were well-

*Gray whale (*Eschrichtius robustus*). This particular whale, distinguished by large orange scars on its back, was first sighted in the waters off the west coast of Vancouver Island in October 1970. For at least the following four years it has been a July-August resident of the same area. The whale is thought to be an older non-breeding male.*

known to the whalers of the early 1800s. As a result, Gray whales were severely depleted by the 1830s. Under protection by international agreement since 1838, the Gray whale has increased and great numbers of these fascinating creatures can be seen passing our shores on their 8,000-mile journey.

In the fall and spring, the whales can be seen passing off the west coast of Vancouver Island en route to winter breeding grounds in the lagoons of southern California and Mexico. The springtime finds this baleen whale travelling north by the same route to summer feeding grounds in the Gulf of Alaska and the Bering Sea where it feeds on the blooming plankton. It is now thought by some biologists that a population of Gray whales, most likely a non-breeding group, remains year round in the region of Pacific Rim National Park.

The Gray whale is slender, with a blunt head and dorsal hump followed by several lesser humps. Its color is mottled grey or blackish, and it has a mature length of 13.5 meters (45 feet).

In sharp contrast to the slow, peaceful and rather drab-colored Gray whale, are the impressive strength, speed and color pattern of the killer whale (*Orcinus orca*). The distinctive white markings on a sleek and solid black background indicate that this species does not need to camouflage its presence from enemies, as there are none.

Killer whales are so called because of their predatory nature. They hunt in packs of three to forty, feeding on fish, birds, seals, sea lions, porpoises and even larger whales. Food is not chewed but is torn into chunks by the powerful jaws and sharp teeth.

Killer whales are distributed worldwide, with their largest concentration thought to be in the Pacific Northwest. They have no definite migration and appear to remain from one season to the next within a loosely established home range. Alert Bay, off the central east coast of Vancouver Island, has perhaps the largest resident killer whale population. Here it is possible to see up to forty animals in a small area. The reason for this concentration is not certain, but it is thought to be connected with the fact that the region is particularly rich in salmon. Haida folklore and art of the Alert Bay region strongly reflect the presence of the killer whale and attest to their presence there for many years.

Killer whales are seen regularly off British Columbia in both open water and within the Straits of Georgia and Juan de Fuca. Occasionally large numbers are seen within Vancouver Harbor. The presence of killer whales in the wild is unmistakable, heralded by what can only be described as powerful exuberance. Leaping and blowing, with large black dorsal fins cutting through the seas, they are a thrilling sight. And while killer whales are not known to prey on humans, they are predators of warm-blooded mammals, and should be respected as such.

Male killer whales grow to 9.15 meters (30 feet) in length, while females remain somewhat smaller at 6.1 to 6.71 meters (20 to 22 feet). The size and shape of the dorsal fin differs in the sexes, the females having a sickle-shaped fin shorter in proportion to body size than the male. The dorsal fin in the male killer whale is triangular in shape and can extend to 1.83 meters (6 feet) in height in a mature bull.

Summer months may find the Pacific white-sided dolphin (*Lagenorhynchus obliquidens*) in British

Columbia waters. This species ranges in the Pacific from California north across the Aleutian chain to Japan, wintering in warmer waters to the south. A big dolphin, up to 2.14 meters (7 feet) in length and 90 to 113.5 kilograms (200 to 250 pounds) in weight, it travels in large groups or pods of up to 2,000 individuals. It is a beautiful dolphin, black on the back with striking light grey sides and white belly. At a distance the Pacific white-sided dolphin may be confused with the Dall's porpoise (*Phocoenoides dalli*) which is colored somewhat like a killer whale — black with large white patches. Unlike Dall's porpoise, Pacific white-sided dolphins are great jumpers and leapers. Dall's porpoises do not jump but they have greater speed and are considered the fastest-swimming of marine mammals, capable of speeds in excess of 40.25 kilometers per hour (25 miles per hour).

The terms "dolphin" and "porpoise" give rise to a great deal of confusion and argument. "Porpoise" is generally used to denote a small cetacean having a blunt nose, spade-shaped teeth and a triangular dorsal fin. "Dolphin" is used in reference to a small cetacean having a beaklike rostrum (snout), needle-like teeth and a sickle-shaped dorsal fin. The words "dolphin" and "porpoise" are actually arbitrary terms. The cetologists (those who study cetaceans) consider "porpoise" to be the more correct for describing small cetaceans, avoiding the confusion between the dolphin mammal and the dolphin fish. "Porpoises" generally do poorly in an oceanarium situation, unlike "dolphins" such as the killer whale and Pacific white-sided dolphin, that do exceptionally well.

The Pacific harbor porpoise (*Phocoena vomerina*) is a relatively common inshore species. It is distinguished from the Pacific white-sided dolphin and the Dall porpoise by having a dark grey to black upper surface with paler belly and no white patches on the sides. This species does not school, rather it travels in small groups of two or four animals. The Risso's dolphin (*Grampus griseus*) is seen less often in the Pacific Northwest, and while the northern right whale dolphin (*Lissodelphis borealis*) and false killer whale (*Pseudorca crassidens*) have not yet been confirmed as occurring off British Columbia, the former has been recorded in Washington and the Bering Sea and the latter in Puget Sound. Other members of the toothed whale group known to occur are the sperm whale (*Physeter catodon*), Baird's beaked whale (*Berardius bairdi*), Cuvier's beaked whale (*Ziphius cavirostris*), Stejneger's beaked whale (*Mesoplodon stegnegeri*) and Hubb's beaked whale (*Mesoplodon carlhubbsi*).

Of the baleen whales other than the previously mentioned Gray whale, the fin whale (*Balaenoptera physalus*), sei whale (*Balaenoptera borealis*), and minke whale (*Balaenoptera acutorostrata*) are known to occur. Rarely seen, as a result of drastically reduced numbers due to overhunting, are the blue whale (*Balaenoptera musculus*), humpback whale (*Megaptera nodosa*), and the very rare North Pacific right whale (*Eubalaena sieboldi*).

While not native to the Pacific Northwest, two very interesting cetaceans of the Arctic regions deserve mention. These are the beluga, or Arctic white whale (*Delphinapterus leucas*), and the narwhal (*Monodon monoceros*). The beluga is snow-white at maturity. At birth this species is a dark mousey-grey, gradually lightening in color to become completely white at three or four years of age. Belugas are classed as toothed whales even though the teeth are mere stubs. This animal feeds by sucking in small crustaceans and bottom fish while foraging on the ocean floor.

The narwhal is similar to the beluga in body shape and size, being approximately 4.58 meters (15 feet) in length. Its color is mottled grey and black. A unique and puzzling feature of this latter species is the development of a long (up to 2.75-meter [9-foot]) straight tusk in the male. Like the beluga, the narwhal is a toothed whale. It is the upper left canine tooth which spirals outward through the lip tissue to produce this unusual tusk. Just why the tusk develops and why generally only in the male is not known.

The narwhal most likely provided the basis for the mythical unicorn, first described in the fourth century B.C., and elaborated by European medieval writers. By the sixteenth century, the spiraled unicorn tusk on the coat of arms of James I of England was remarkably similar in every respect to that of the narwhal.

It is possible that many readers will never experience the thrill of seeing a whale or dolphin in the wild, but perhaps just knowing that these creatures are there, beneath the rippled surface of the sea, is reason enough to be awed by their being.

Suggested Reading

GENERAL

Carefoot, Tom. *Seashore Ecology*. Vancouver: J. J. Douglas, (in Press), 1976.

Johnson, M. E. and Snook, H. J. *Seashore Animals of the Pacific Coast*. New York: Dover Publications Inc., Dover Edition, 1967.

Kozloff, Eugene N. *Seashore Life of Puget Sound, the Strait of Georgia and the San Juan Archipelago*. Vancouver: J. J. Douglas Ltd., 1973.

MacGintie, G. E. and MacGintie, Nettie. *Natural History of Marine Animals*. New York: McGraw-Hill Book Co. Inc., 1949.

McConnaughey, Bayard H. *Introduction to Marine Biology*. Second Edition. St. Louis: C. V. Mosby Company, 1974.

Ricketts, E. F. and Calvin, Jack. *Between Pacific Tides*. Fourth Edition, edited by Joel W. Hedgpeth. Stanford: Stanford University Press, 1968.

INVERTEBRATE KEYS

Kozloff, Eugene N. *Keys to the Marine Invertebrates of Puget Sound, the San Juan Archipelago and Adjacent Regions*. Seattle: University of Washington Press, 1974.

Smith, Ralph I. and Carlton, James T., ed. *Lights Manual*. Third Edition. Berkeley: University of California Press. 1975.

SEAWEEDS

Scagel, Robert. *Guide to Common Seaweeds of British Columbia*. Handbook 27, B.C. Provincial Museum, 1976.

INVERTEBRATES

Abbott, R. Tucker. *American Sea Shells*. Toronto: Van Nostrand Reinhold, 1974.

Cornwall, Ira E. *The Barnacles of British Columbia*. Handbook 7, B.C. Provincial Museum, 1955.

Furlong, Marjorie and Pill, Virginia. *Starfish, Guides to Identification and Methods of Preserving*. Second Edition. Ellis Robinson Publishing Company Inc., 1972.

Griffith, Lela M. *Intertidal Univalves of British Columbia*. Handbook 26, B.C. Provincial Museum, 1967.

Milne, Lorus and Margery. *Invertebrates of North America*. New York: Doubleday & Co. Inc., no date.

Quayle, D. B. *Intertidal Bivalves of British Columbia*. Handbook 17, B.C. Provincial Museum, 1960.

Rice, Tom. *Marine Shells of the Pacific Northwest*. Ellis Robinson Publishing Co. Ltd., 1972.

Schmitt, Waldo L. *The Marine Decapod Crustacea of California*. University of California Publication, 1921.

FISH

Hart, J. L. *Pacific Fishes of Canada*. Fisheries Research Board Bulletin 180, 1973.

Herald, Earl. *Fishes of North America*. New York: Doubleday & Co. Inc., no date.

Herald, Earl S. *Living Fishes of the World*. New York: Doubleday & Co. Inc., 1972.

Marshall, N. B. *The Life of Fishes*. London: Weidenfeld and Nicolson, 1965.

Norman, J. R. *A History of Fishes*. Third Edition by P. H. Greenwood. London: Ernest Benn Ltd., 1975.

Walford, Lionel A. *Marine Game Fishes of the Pacific Coast from Alaska to the Equator*. © 1937. Reprinted 1974 for the Smithsonian Institution by T. F. H. Publications, Inc., New Jersey.

MARINE MAMMALS

Daugherty, Anita. *Marine Mammals of California*. California Department of Fish & Game, First Revision, 1966.

Harrison, R. J. and King, Judith E. *Marine Mammals*. London: Hutchinson & Co. Ltd., 1965.

Kenyon, Karl W. *The Sea Otter in the Eastern Pacific Ocean*. New York: Dover Publications Inc., 1975.

Leatherwood, Steve, Evans, W. E. and Rice, Dale W. *The Whales, Dolphins, and Porpoises of the Eastern North Pacific*. Naval Undersea Research and Development Center, San Diego.

Pacific Research Books. *Baleen Whales: In Eastern North Pacific and Arctic Waters*. Seattle: 1971.

Pacific Research Books. *Seals, Sea Lions, Walruses: In Eastern North Pacific and Arctic Waters*. Seattle: 1972.

Pacific Research Books. *Toothed Whales in Eastern North Pacific Waters*. Seattle: 1971.

Peterson, Richard S. and Bartholomew, George A. *The Natural History and Behaviour of the California Sea Lion*. Special Publication No. 1, The American Society of Naturalists, 1967.

Pike, G. C. and MacAskie, I. *Marine Mammals of British Columbia*. Fisheries Research Board of Canada, Bulletin 171, 1969.

Scheffer, Victor B. *Seals, Sea Lions and Walruses*. Stanford: Stanford University Press, 1958.

Slijper, E. J. *Whales*. London: Hutchinson & Co. Ltd. 1962.

Wood, Forrest G. *Marine Mammals and Man*. Washington: Robert B. Luce, Inc. 1973.

BIRDS ASSOCIATED WITH THE COAST

Beebe, F. L. *Field Studies of the Falconiformes of British Columbia*. Victoria: B.C. Provincial Museum occasional paper #17, 1974.

Bellrose, F. C. *Ducks, Geese and Swans of North America*. Pennsylvania: Stackpole Books, 1975.

Gabrielson, I. N. and Lincoln, F. C. *The Birds of Alaska*. Pennsylvania: Stackpole Books, 1959.

Godfrey, W. E. *The Birds of Canada*. National Museum of Canada, Bulletin #203, 1966.

Hatler, D. F., Campbell, R. W. and Dorst, E. A. *Birds of Pacific Rim National Park, B.C.* Victoria: B.C. Provincial Museum occasional papers, 1976.

Jewett, S. G., Taylor, W. D., Shaw, W. T. and Aldertigh, J. W. *Birds of Washington State*. Seattle: University of Washington Press, 1953.

Larrison, E. J. and Sonnenberg, K. G. *Western Birds: Their Location and Identification*. Seattle Audubon Society, 1968.

Munro, J. A. and Cowan, McTaggart. *A Review of the Bird Fauna of B.C.* Victoria: B.C. Provincial Museum Special Publication, #2, 1974.

Peterson, R. T. *A Field Guide to Western Birds*. Boston: Houghton Mifflin Co., 1961.

Robbins, C. S., Bruun, P. and Zim, H. S. *Birds of North America: A Guide to Field Identification*. New York: Golden Press, 1966.

Small, A. *Birds of California*. New York: Winchester Press, 1974.

Vancouver Natural History Society. *Nature West Coast: As seen in Lighthouse Park*. Vancouver: Discovery Press, 1973.

Index

175